£ 12

(1238)

BIRD LIFE IN TWO DELTAS

BIRD LIFE
IN TWO DELTAS

*Being the diaries of a bird
photographer in the estuaries
of the Guadalquiver & the Rhone
& their neighbourhoods*

by

G. K. YEATES

B.A., F.R.P.S.

FABER AND FABER LIMITED
24 Russell Square
London

First published in Mcmxlvi
by Faber and Faber Limited
24 Russell Square London W.C.1
Printed in Great Britain by
Western Printing Services Limited Bristol

TO RUPERT
my Springer Spaniel,
a very dear and faithful friend,
who was born on the day on which
I photographed the Night Heron

CONTENTS

MAPS

ILLUSTRATIONS

ILLUSTRATIONS

ILLUSTRATIONS

PREFACE

THE official list of British birds contains many species which owe their inclusion to the 'honour' of a single obituary notice or to merely casual vagrancy. On that account and by frequent repetition in our text books these rarities have become familiar as mere names even to those who take only a passing interest in birds. Have we not all indeed passed through the phase when every kestrel was a lesser kestrel, and every grey heron was thought to have purple on its long neck? Although we have never seen these birds, nor are likely to, within the confines of our own islands, we are, because of the full treatment they receive in our handbooks, almost unreasonably familiar with them, their plumage and their ways. They are part of our background and of our knowledge to an illogical degree.

If the mere name and coloured plate of the text book are ever to have any reality in the flesh, it is necessary to travel abroad—to the Continent and beyond. Many bird watchers are dissuaded from this in the mistaken idea that once across the Channel so many new species will appear that confusion and chaos in identification will result. There will be new species, of course, birds which have never even wandered to Britain, but it is not until a bird trip abroad has been undertaken that it is truly realized how many of the birds of Western Europe are included on the British list, and how few there are with which one has not at least a nodding acquaintance from our own bird books. Indeed, apart from the excitement and delight of seeing, often in abundance, birds which have until then been merely names, a European bird trip is a very necessary stage in the development of a British ornithologist, if he is to get in proper proportion a panorama of the bird-life of his own islands. This book is the record of a bird photographer's visits to two great European bird haunts with the

[13]

avowed object of seeing in life some of the many names with which from boyhood he had been familiar.

The Spanish *marismas* at the estuary of the great Guadalquiver and the Camargue or Rhône-Delta constitute two of the greatest bird paradises in Western Europe. The brief visits of a foreigner to these great oases of bird-life, so vast that even a lifetime would leave much unseen and unexplored, can in themselves provide only a fleeting glimpse into the wealth and variety of their natural history. These three diaries which follow are the unadorned records of my visits. I have left them as diaries, the daily accounts of what I actually saw and did, because I hope that that method of treatment will reveal more forcibly the amazing variety of the avifauna of these two ornithological Meccas.

In the pages which follow I would ask the reader to bear in mind that they are field notes, written at the time and altered only where the clipped style and the incomplete and ungrammatical sentence of the diary would in their original form have been irritating to a degree, and that the mistakes and false conclusions of the moment have been left as they were originally made and corrected only in footnotes; that when I visited the Camargue, my sources of reference for estimating the status of any given species were not then (1937 and 1938) in the advanced state into which the papers of Mayaud (1938) and Glegg (1941) have since brought out knowledge (see Bibliography).

My debts of gratitude are numerous. I must thank Mr. B. W. Tucker and Mr. H. J. R. Pease for inviting me to join their Andalucian expedition, and above all for the help given to me in the identification of many birds which I was seeing for the first time, of many indeed with which I had not been even on nodding acquaintance. An ornithologist's first European venture must needs occasionally find him at a loss, especially if it be to Southern Spain where a few North African species further confuse the issue. With two such excellent and experienced cicerones I was indeed fortunate in my introduction to our rare birds abroad. The experience and knowledge gained in Spain at their hands enabled me to stand on my own feet in the Camargue. How well they performed their tutorship can be judged by the fact that in two visits to Provence I only once found myself completely beaten by a bird—an immature red-footed falcon.

Mr. B. W. Tucker I must also thank for permission to reproduce seven scenic photographs which he took at the time of our visit, and which bear his name in the list of illustrations.

In the Camargue I was accompanied on my first visit by Mr. A. S. Phillips whom I must thank not only for the good company which is so important a part of the enjoyment of a bird trip, but also for the very real and often laborious help which he gave me in the construction of my photographic hides, particularly in the case of the little egret. I can only hope that he found some consolation for the buffeting of the mistral and the attacks of the mosquitoes in the excellent film which he himself took at the same time.

The following year I was accompanied by Mr. H. A. Patrick and Mr. M. G. Robinson, and them I would also thank for their many good services and industry on my behalf and for their most amusing companionship.

Nor can I possibly fail to mention the kindness and courtesy of the Director of the Camargue Reserve, Dr. G. Tallon of Arles, without whose efforts and anxiety to help much would have remained as forbidden and unknown ground. Perhaps not the least of my debts of gratitude to him are his patience and forbearance with my execrable French grammar and pronunciation with which I must have offended him on the many occasions of our evening councils of war! His *gardes*, Mon. Lomont, of Salin de Badon, and Mon. Bouisset, of La Capelière, were most helpful and hospitable. The latter indeed was indefatigable and was even prepared to engage in wordy war on my behalf. To Mon. Malaza, of Marseilles, I owe thanks not only for the generous manner in which he permitted me to invade his property at Les Grandes Cabanes to work black-winged stilts, but more especially for his trust in giving me that permission on the mere evidence of a short telegram from an unknown Englishman!

I hope that the end of the war finds one and all of the above gentlemen safe and sound, and that the Camargue will once again flourish as a great Mecca of bird-life. At the moment of writing my latest reports from France indicate that the French Army is proposing to make it a military training ground. As a

[15]

mere foreigner who was once a guest to its *étangs* and *marais*, I hope and pray that it will be left to my hosts in its original state in order that they may invite me again!

The photographs which accompany the text were, with the exception only of those of the bittern and of Montagu's harrier, all taken on the occasions and in the circumstances described in the diaries of my activities. On this account a few which were also reproduced in my last book, *Bird Photography*, have had to be reproduced again in the present volume.

G. K. YEATES

Norwich,
  November 1945.

AN ANDALUCIAN DIARY

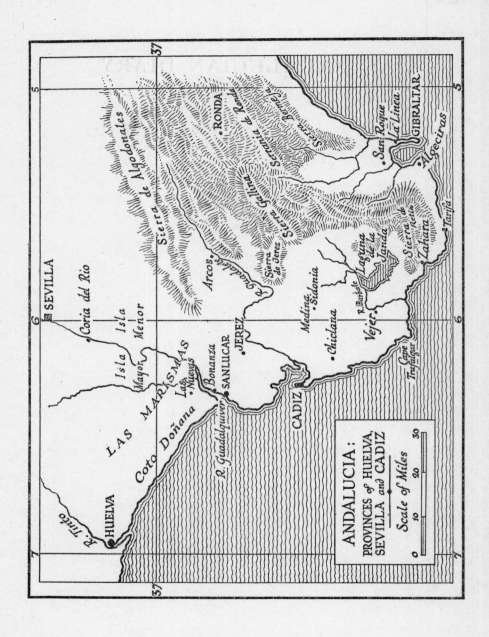

ANDALUCIA:
PROVINCES of HUELVA,
SEVILLA and CADIZ

Scale of Miles
0   10   20   30

AN ANDALUCIAN DIARY

APRIL 9TH. At 10 a.m. the *Comorin* landed me at Gibraltar.
When at last the business of getting ashore was over, I still had
two hours to wait before picking up T. and P. at the Bristol. So I
pottered about the long narrow street that forms the nerve centre
of the Rock, initiated myself into the intricacies of Spanish
finance, looked at such of the Fleet as lay in the harbour, bought
the necessary odds and ends which had been omitted in the
hurry of departure, looked up some friends, and generally behaved like a good tourist. Eventually I found my way to the
Bristol where in the gardens I was greeted by a blackbird. I
thought Spain might have been more enterprising in its first
bird! But I suppose it was very much in character that so
English a species should greet a Britisher in this important out-
post of Empire.

T. and P. duly arrived in the V.8. Lunch over and my hide,
camera, and self with no little difficulty packed away, we set off
for Spain proper. We had soon left the last English 'bobby' behind, were across the narrow neck of no man's land which
separates Gib. from Spain, and had drawn up at the customs at
La Linea. Prying officials dipped into the car, examined my
camera with much suspicion, and finally finished by charging
me with the Spanish equivalent of a pound for the many boxes
of plates with which my suitcase was liberally encumbered. At
last we could start in earnest.

Nor were we long about it. Soon after San Roque in some low
pastureland to the left of the road a flock of snowy white birds
were dancing attendance upon a herd of cattle. Dancing is the
right word, for as the cows moved, their satellites jumped and
skipped out of their cumbrous way. When the beasts settled down
again, the birds again ran eagerly round their legs and about
their lowered heads. The glasses revealed them as buff-backed

[19]

herons. I must confess that these were so white that the name seemed something of a misnomer, and had it not been for their pink beaks and legs, I should have unhesitatingly put them down as little egrets. But the egret stalks about on black legs, nor has it this helpful characteristic of dancing attendance on cattle.[1] Buff-backs they were, without a doubt, lacking as yet the buff plumes on head, breast, and back which are the full breeding plumage of this African heron.

I took my camera from the car, fitted the telephoto lens, and started to stalk them. I soon found that the problem was not to find a tame buff-back, but to locate a tame cow. Always it was the cattle which took fright first, and with them went the herons. But at last I got a few exposures, and one or two also of a group of birds as they stood idly by in the shade of a clump of eucalyptus, and singularly lovely they looked in this setting.

Thence into Algeciras, which I shall remember chiefly for the smell of fish. Never did even Billingsgate rival it! After tea we attracted some curiosity by standing in the street and examining through our glasses the hordes of swifts which hurtled past our heads and over the roof-tops. We were looking for a pallid swift, but our efforts were unrewarded. Not only did the gaping curiosity of the crowd become embarrassing, but the brilliance of the light made suspect any identification of a species which differs from the common swift only in the paleness of its brown plumage.

We continued our journey on to Tarifa. The road was now running through low foothills covered with cistus, dwarf gorse, and a tangle of scrub and rocks. Cork oaks were the characteristic trees, often clinging on with precarious foothold. Many small birds were flitting about, and I soon realized that there were going to be many birds to which I was going to find it difficult to put a name. It was with some relief therefore that I noted swallows flying overhead, and on the wires corn buntings churning out their unmusical songs just as they do on English pastures. Then a bee-eater flashed by—a gorgeous medley of greens and yellows. But I did not see it well. Near Tarifa some griffon vultures were circling over a distant crag, mere specks in the sky,

[1] The French name for the buff-backed heron is particularly happy—*Héron garde-boeufs*.

PLATE 2. BUFF-BACKED HERONS FEEDING
A typical Andalucian scene in April, showing the characteristic association of these herons with cattle

PLATE 1. BUFF-BACKED HERONS IN THE FIELDS
A small flock seeking for insects in the shade of eucalyptus

PLATE 3. THE MIGHTY WINGS OF THE GRIFFON VULTURE

but even at that distance their characteristic square shape gave them away.

We were now bound for Vejer, our first headquarters, and although evening was drawing in, we stopped for a while on the edge of the lagoon of La Janda, here quite close to the road. As we moved through the fringe of cork oaks, bee-eaters were everywhere seeking their insect prey. A man may be forgiven if on first seeing a bee-eater he sits down and wipes his brow. For how can one adequately describe that brilliance of yellow throat, green breast, and chestnut-gold back? If it was the rainbow that gave the kingfisher birth, what palette of nature's ever mixed the gorgeous riot of brilliant colour wherein the bee-eater is painted? Each hue and tone is plastered on without stint. The yellow on the throat is brightest yellow; no greens are brighter than a bee-eater's greens, no chestnuts richer in tone. Such brilliance and such contrasts would in human hands produce nothing but harshness and vulgarity. But the bee-eater is neither harsh nor vulgar. It is a singularly lovely bird. Seen as we saw them to-day with every colour ablaze in the sun against a sky so blue that no artist would dare paint its depth for fear of exaggeration, they were more gorgeous than any plate in any bird book had given me to believe—except one, W. H. Riddell's lovely thing of bee-eaters in flight in Abel Chapman's last book, *Memories*. I bought that book very largely just for the sake of that painting—and to-day I have seen the living image of it, save that instead of six birds our flocks were ten or fifteen strong. They were brighter almost than the sun which blazed upon them. But truly what is it in the pigment functions of living things which can produce on the one hand, in one species such as this, a feast of colour so rich and yet on the other side, in birds like the corn buntings we passed by the roadside, a colour scheme so dull that it is impossible to enthuse? What purpose does it serve, and why the difference?

They were flying in small flocks just over the tops of the cork-oaks, looking rather like big green swallows with unusually long pointed tails. They fly in bursts, quick wing-beats and then long glides, and all the time their cheerful, liquid notes resound. Periodically a flock would perch on the cork oaks.

At the edge of the cork trees a pair of woodchat shrikes were staking out their territory. Lovely indeed is that bright chestnut head, with the bold black stripe through the eye and the marked black and white patterning of the back. His lady was a more subdued edition of himself, but not in any way so different as in the sexes of our own red-backed shrike.

As we emerged through the cork oaks on to the high ground above the lagoon a wheatear caught my eye. It was of the black-eared species with a fine light head, black cheeks and buff shoulders and breast—definitely the white-throated variety of this dimorphic wheatear. But soon my eyes were wandering on to the *vega* of the La Janda. Here were numerous white storks standing at rest, and, joy of joys, close to us a pair of common cranes were parading with long elegant strides. Their soft grey plumage and their drooping plumes are indeed lovely, and our views of them were perfect. Over the reed beds marsh harriers were drifting, and a great flight of mallard rose from the hidden waters.

But we could not stay for more. This visit was in the nature of a reconnaissance, and it was certainly successful. We returned to the car for the last lap. Even so before we set forth, we saw yet another fine bird. On a fence post, from which it boomeranged into the air like a huge flycatcher after its prey, sat a bird the size of a jackdaw, with a breast of the most vivid blue and a back of richest chestnut—a roller in all his glory. Recovering from the shock (for it was little less), we proceeded on the way. If this is but the first six hours of Spain, what will the next three weeks reveal?

At last, Vejer came into sight up a long avenue of cork oaks. It is difficult adequately to give due praise to the appearance of Vejer, for it stands on a height over the Barbate river, a veritable Spanish eyrie with its whitewashed jumble of houses sparkling in the evening sun. The V.8 had to climb a long winding track which eventually led us to the local pub, where three tired men went to bed after a filthy dinner of Spanish grease to the accompaniment of the pleasant music of castanettes in the village square beneath.

APRIL 10TH. I woke early to find the sun streaming in at the window. On the bare, whitewashed wall of the house opposite was a lesser kestrel, clinging on to a small crevice and chattering noisily. I picked up the telescope, propped up my pillow and in my pyjamas, if you please, settled down to watch a new species!

The lesser kestrel, the male at least, is the image of our own bird, with one very decisive and diagnostic exception. The rich red mantle is unspotted. I thought too that his colours were brighter, particularly the blues of his head and tail, but in this bright Mediterranean light one might expect this to be the case. As to size, he may be slightly smaller than our bird, but even if the two were seen together, I feel that with size alone as a guide they would need careful separation.

The hen bird very obligingly arrived. I could see no difference at all between her and the female of the true kestrel, unless perhaps she was cleaner in her colours. The chattering of the cock, however, although very like the excited *kee-kee-kee* of our bird, is to my ear definitely much shriller and higher pitched.

The gods of the chase were in benign mood this morning. Not content with granting me one new bird as I lay in my pyjamas, they handed me a second. A starling intruded, perching on an old window-sill near the kestrels. But this was no English starling, for it lacked all those iridescent spots and was dull and lifeless in its tones. It could only be the spotless or Sardinian starling—but a starling by any other name is just as dull! I think the only starling which could excite me would be the rose-coloured pastor.

After breakfast, we found the V.8 punctured, so had to change the wheel before starting. The departure from the pub was most awe-inspiring. Half the town turned out to see us—shaggy-looking gentlemen with sombreros on their heads and cylindrical trousers on their nether portions. They stood and stared, crowds of them, and never a word was spoken—most embarrassing. I was not sorry when the car was heading down the twisting road that connects Vejer with the main Gibraltar-Cadiz highway. Half-way down a low tree, as yet unleaved, but clad in brilliant pink blossom caught my eye—a Judas tree, I believe. My botany is poor. Anyway, it was lovely beyond words.

The original intention was La Janda, but the puncture made us first find a garage. At Vejer they did not play mending punctures at the local garage. Too much like work for a Spaniard, I imagine. So we had to take the Cadiz direction. Petrol pumps were fairly frequent, but repairs . . . well, perhaps to-morrow. My Spanish is negligible, but nobody who comes to Andalucia can fail to hear the word *mañana*. Truly these Spaniards are close students of Macbeth. *Mañana* is the middle name of the Andalucian. After only twenty-four hours I can see that everything is put off till to-morrow, and in view of the heat I can readily understand it too.

Twenty miles on, at Chiclana, we eventually found a garage prepared to get straight down to the work. In the meantime I took a leaf out of the Spaniards' book. I siesta-ed. In that blazing sun I pondered two weighty thoughts: (*a*) why does this sun-baked people choose whitewash for its house colouring (even through dark glasses I had a headache), and (*b*) why in such a thirst-making land is the national drink a short one? Sherry has its points . . . but so has beer.

This diversion cost us the morning, but it was not wasted ornithologically. En route we stopped to examine a superb cock Montagu's harrier quartering a field. His black-tipped blue wings flashed in the sun—a lovely sight. More griffons were in the distance—still bad views. A black kite gave us a fleeting glimpse. It looked very dark, but I did not see it well. A pair of little owls sat on a telegraph pole, looking so attractive that for the moment I could readily understand the motives which had prompted Lilford & Co. to introduce it to Britain.

I saw my first crested larks—very sandy in colour. T. tells me it is a pale sub-species, this crested lark of Andalucia. Certainly it was a very washed-out specimen; otherwise very like a skylark, but with rounded wings. The crest is very conspicuous when raised, but when flat on the crown (where it usually is), does not help very much in identification.

The crested lark position down here is very confusing, because there is a distinct species, Brehm's crested lark, which one cannot really identify till it is dead! At least it has a different wing formula and a thicker bill. Not very helpful as field characters. If it were merely a sub-species, one would not mind, but as a definite species it is rather irritating not to be sure which it is you are looking at—the ordinary crested or Herr Brehm's edition.

The ubiquitous corn bunting was everywhere. So too were the

buff-backed herons, at least wherever there were cattle. One played its role of cattle egret properly by standing on a cow's back. Stonechats and whinchats were both frequent on the wires. But I was chiefly interested in the Spanish yellow wagtail. We get so used to these geographical sub-species that many field ornithologists are inclined to overlook them, but the prefix Spanish does not mean that this wagtail looks precisely like our yellow wagtail. On the contrary it is really a blue-headed wagtail. It had a very well-defined eye stripe and a very white chin. More it is difficult to say in a field identification. It was a most lovely bird.

At last we had retraced our steps and were back at La Janda. The lagoon is certainly a surprise. On the map it is marked as a big expanse of water, but as one views it from the edge of the cork oaks the land falls away over a flat level (*vega* is the technical name) onto what looks like a vast plain. Beyond the sierras rise in rugged mass. At first I thought the place dry, but a closer inspection showed that in fact the whole area was flooded to a depth of about two feet, the water being hidden by the density of the reed growth.

By the time we reached the water I was so hot that wading was a pleasure. But it was undoubtedly a profitless task ploughing through those reeds. About head high, they very effectively cut off one's view, and the leeches which lurked in the water did their best to spoil the fun.

In this reed forest we saw coots and dabchicks. There were also reed warblers, both common and great. Try as I would, I could not get good views of this last species. Mallard were everywhere, and three widgeon were noted, but except for a disputed pintail little else in the duck line revealed itself. An incredible row up-marsh proved itself to be the chorus of a pair of cranes. A big flock of whiskered terns came past us. At first these may easily be taken for black terns, but their white cheeks quickly distinguished them, while the black of their underparts is not so dark.

We emerged from the depths and sat in the shade of a bush just above the water line. A little ring plover very kindly came down to the water's edge. Its legs were less bright than the orange ones we are accustomed to see in our bird. Again, when it flew, it was without any white wing bar. It looked altogether a more frail wee bird. Four green sandpipers then added to the fun, and, just before we left, a tawny pipit came very close indeed. A rather large and very slim pipit this; distinctly wagtail-like in stance and shape. It was almost completely unspotted on the breast and very soberly marked on the back. The stripes over the eye and beneath the bill on to the throat were so marked as to give the impression that it had a dark moustache. Its legs, too, were very pale.

We now made our way back through the cork oaks to the road. Cicadas and tree frogs were very noisy. I got my first view of an Egyptian vulture. The black and white patterning on the wings is very like that of a stork, with which bird alone it can be confused when in flight. But the wedge-shaped tail and the head, retracted in typical vulture fashion into the ruff, immediately pick it out, for the stork's neck straggles out. Yet at a distance they can be confusing.

A pair of woodchats were busy at their courting. The cock assumed some strange postures. In front of the female he drew himself up to full height, until he looked twice his normal length. Then he bobbed his head up and down. It was as though he was on a spring which kept alternately shooting him out and drawing him in—a Jack-in-the-box in perpetual motion. Every now and then he quivered his wings. He had, too, a delightful little song.

The last bird of note to-day was an orphean warbler, and of it I got grand views. It is at first sight a large blackcap, but the black of the head runs further down the nape and ends uncertainly; without any definite boundary it merges into the grey-brown of the back. The underparts seemed to be buff, and the contrast between the black head and the white throat very strongly marked.

When we got to the curved bridge over the Barbate at the foot of the crag on which Vejer is built, the usual pair of civil guards stopped the car. We are getting used to this infernal curiosity. Everywhere they stop us and inquire our business. This same gentleman had pulled us up last night on our arrival—quite justifiably no doubt. He had done so again on our way through at lunch time; now he was at it again. Sheer officiousness this time, and all the more infuriating because on this occasion he stuck his head under the hood and belched garlic and onions at a foot range straight into my face. I spluttered with indignation. T. burst out laughing. *Civil* guards seems a fine name![1]

I am much intrigued by the Spanish 'police'. These genuine articles are half soldiers, usually in pairs, decked up in the most incredible garments—green jackets, with yellow Sam Brownes, and yellow slings to their rifles, black boots, and the most ridiculous black hats. There is a lesser order of policeman garbed in 'blues' and with a sword. I cannot for the life of me make out how the business works. A spot of observation on the habits of the two species might be interesting when we get a moment's rest from watching birds. For the moment, however, I am not anxious for another dose of garlic.

APRIL 11TH. This morning we took the road (?) to Casas Viejas on the way to Medina Sidonia. (Did the gentleman of Armada fame, I wonder, come from here?) Our objective was the top end of La Janda. This was some way from the road, and we followed a stream which meandered through deep scrub and tangles of ilex and eucalyptus. Twice I ran straight into a bull round the corner. The beasts looked far too much like African buffalo in such surroundings and I gave them as wide a berth as with dignity I could manage.

La Janda here at its northern end is narrower, less densely reeded; the water shallower, and the bird life more varied. Leeches were also more common. I was glad of my gum boots especially when I saw the hordes which surrounded P. T., although naked of leg, was left completely untouched! Comment superfluous!

Harriers, both marsh and Montagu, were very numerous. Everywhere they were quartering the ground. I sat down to watch them, for where before have I had such opportunities for observation? The lovely grey-blues of the Montagu cocks show little variety, but the marsh vary greatly. All these last have light golden heads, but the buff on the shoulders varies considerably in extent. In certain specimens it was only slight. In others there

[1] At the time of this incident, when this was written, I did not know that 'the suspicions' of the *Guardia Civil* had been aroused by three British bird photographers after griffon vultures near Tarifa just before my arrival. See R. Atkinson, *Quest for the Griffon*—a most amusing and readable book.

was so much of it that the whole bird seemed almost piebald. They were slowly and deliberately quartering the ground, as numerous as a flock of sea-swallows at a ternery, usually low over the reeds. When they pounce, they do not drop in directly, but like a barn owl swing round in a small circle and pounce 'back' to seize their prey. At times, if they are not immediately successful in making contact, they hop along the ground clutching at the grass clumps trying to catch the unwilling mouse which has eluded their ruthless swoop.

As soon as we entered the water, mallard left in swarms, and two cranes were flushed. This pair was immediately joined by three more, and for some minutes they circled round trumpeting loudly before they made off down the lagoon. They fly like storks with their long necks stretched out, slightly drooped, and not tucked up like herons.

Almost immediately I got my first good view of griffon vulture, for a pair sailed slowly overhead—majestic beyond words in their effortless flight. The griffon in the air is extraordinarily oblong shaped. His vast wings are not cut away as in other birds. The front and hind parts are parallel and only the separated tips of the primaries break the symmetry of his outline. The tail, too, is square and protrudes but little beyond the body; likewise the head and neck which are tucked into the white ruff. He is dark brown beneath, save that from either side of the body towards the wing tips two light lines radiate.

From the huge griffon to the small Savi's warbler seemed an absurd transfer, but this last species was the real object of our visit to this part of La Janda. We could hear them reeling in the reeds, and proceeded to stalk. They were very obliging, for unlike their furtive relative, the grasshopper warbler, they sat out openly when reeling on the reed stems. Our views were excellent.

Savi's warbler in general shape resembles the grasshopper. The tail is typically bulbous, but I was struck by the angle at which it was carried, firmly depressed against the reed stem, thus making a very abrupt angle between the back and the tail. The whole bird, too, lacks the dark streakings of the grasshopper, being uniform brown all over. Although there were several pairs present, they were very localized in their distribution. All were

PLATE 4. SCRUB COUNTRY NEAR VEJER

This is the characteristic scrub country of the Andalucian foothills, the habitat of many small birds, particularly Orphean Warblers and Woodchat Shrikes. Vejer in background

PLATE 5. SIERRA DE RETIN, NEAR ZAHARA

A typical outcrop in the Sierras, and a characteristic habitat of the Black Wheatear

PLATE 6. TWO FULL-FED GRIFFON VULTURES

PLATE 7. THE FOUL FEAST—GRIFFON VULTURES AT CARCASS

found in a very wet area just at the edge of the main reed beds, but always where a rank mat of rough sedge growth made a floating carpet over the deep water.

In this same habitat were also many purple herons. This species is well named, for a dark purple suffuses the whole bird, and the neck is strongly bronzed and very thin. Indeed, it looks like a darker, but very much more slender, grey heron. The colony was wheeling above the reed bed and calling in alarm. I could see very little difference between their alarm notes and the familiar *franks* of an English heronry. The birds clearly had nests, and a search soon produced one, a very substantial, well banked-up platform of reeds in which were four typical heron blue eggs. All the obstructing reed stems in the vicinity of the nest had been carefully bent over by the birds.

This search had driven a marsh harrier into a state of frantic panic, so we set to work on this, and soon located a nest with five white eggs. Here again, as in the purple heron, the nest was very substantially constructed, and I was, above all, surprised at the depth of water above which it was sited.

Where the reeds alternated with the rough grass at the edge of the lagoon, a fantail warbler was building its nest. The spiders' webs were clearly visible in its beak, but we failed to locate the nest—much to my disappointment, for this *Cisticola* is amongst the most remarkable of bird architects.

Finally, on our way back, from the depths of the undergrowth of the small stream a powerful outburst of song attracted immediate attention, so commanding was its volume. Cetti's warbler is more often heard than seen, and on this occasion I never so much as managed to glimpse the songster in the dense tangle of the stream-side.

APRIL 12TH. I spent the morning on the roof of the hotel, watching lesser kestrels and spotless starlings, and trying to get some flight pictures of the former. T. and P. went off on their own devices. We were to meet on the bridge for lunch.

The hotel roof makes a magnificent observation post for the kestrels. Behind are old courtyards, and, immediately attached, an old house with the roof no longer extant. The walls of both courtyards and house are pitted and scarred, where bricks have fallen away, thus forming the crannies and holes which are the delight of the lesser kestrel.

When I poked my head over, six or seven pairs were clinging on to the wall face, chattering away noisily, staking out their claims to nesting sites, for breeding has not yet begun. Apart from the pairs occupying this particular place there were literally hundreds flying about over the town, and as they hunted for insects round the church, I could not help comparing them to swifts round an English spire in August. Not that there is very much real resemblance, except that the lesser kestrel also flies with a few rapid wing beats and then long sweeping glides. To-day I saw one for the first time hovering over the water meadows in true kestrel fashion, but they do not do so as frequently as our bird.

The efforts at flight pictures were not a success. Whenever I stuck the lens of the camera over the side of the house, I was greeted with a storm of what at least sounded like barbarian abuse from a family engaged in its washing in the courtyard, and who seemed to regard my innocent scrambles as curiosity into their affairs. The man looked such a cut-throat that I deemed it wise to keep in the background. However, I was rewarded by finding the nest of a spotless starling. It held four eggs, much the same as our bird's, and the nest was typically untidy. The site interested me, for it was placed in a hole which had no protection from the sky. Most hole-nesting birds use sites which are sheltered from the rain. This fellow must catch the full blast of any rain storm. The reason, of course, is that it just does not rain here, so that the bird need take no thought for such matters. To-day has been scorching, and it is difficult to believe that it is ever anything else.

At noon I wandered down to the bridge, inspecting en route the crag beneath the town from which eagle owls have been reported—but I had no luck. I admired with childish delight the spectacle of lemons growing. Thence to the bridge where the belching civil guard was still on duty. From the curiosity of his stare I lived in ready anticipation of another blast of garlic. Fortunately T. and P. arrived in time.

We took our lunch down to the coast at Zahara in readiness for a trip into the Sierra de Retin in search of Bonelli's eagle.

Here we were treated to a ludicrous exhibition of pig-driving. Zahara lay across the estuary and was connected to us by a wooden bridge. From its streets a man appeared with about a dozen pigs, which apparently he wanted to get over to our side. The bridge seemed to me a perfectly good means of communication, but the swineherd thought differently. Perhaps they do not allow pigs to use bridges in Spain. Anyway, the eye of the law was upon him, for one of the lesser order of policemen, of the blue-uniformed, besworded brigade, was watching him. The pigs were unceremoniously booted, good and hard, into the water. The recalcitrant were treated to a kick in the mouth. Once in the water, they were discouraged from returning by a barrage of stones. This was apparently the signal for the village to turn out for the fun. Quite a dozen people now picked up a bosom-load of stones and from the bridge, keeping up with the unfortunate pigs, liberally plastered their behinds with much shouting and noise. Rather to my surprise the pigs arrived safely but with obvious relief. More boots encouraged them down the road, and they vanished. What a life!

We now started up into the sierra—terribly rough going over boulders and through stubborn cistus. Almost immediately I was rewarded with a new bird—a black wheatear, and a fine cock in deepest black up to the clean white rump. He looked large as he skipped about the rocks, but he had all the mannerisms of our bird.

Our energetic scrambles into the heights were not visited by much success. Yet that sierra side will always remain a vivid picture in my mind, if only for the indescribable loveliness of its flowers. Yellows, whites, blues, covered the slopes in the greatest profusion—a joy to the eye. They were not such a joy to the touch, for their prickles cut even through breeches. What T. and P., who were in shorts and grey flannels, thought of them is not repeatable.

Plodding up through the scrub I flushed a Dartford warbler from a nest with three eggs. This is the Spanish form of our bird, supposedly more grey above, but I cannot say I was impressed by the distinction. There were quite a few griffons about, and in the widely spaced crags around I doubt not that they were nesting. I saw one bird sitting on a crevice on a huge lone pinnacle of rock, quite inaccessible. I could not see a nest, but it might easily have been tucked away amongst the ledges. I clapped my hands and in wonderful majesty the vulture spread its mighty wings and swept away.

On the eastern side of the sierra we flushed two Egyptian vultures from crevices. Both of these I reached, and both held what looked like old nests, and probably were, for *Neophron* is a much later-breeding bird than the January-nesting griffon. An unholy smell was attached to the ledges. I got good views of them here, and I must agree that when at rest they are peculiarly unsavoury-looking birds, with their naked yellow faces and their scruffy frills round their heads. The whites that predominate on their plumage are truly frowsy. In the air it is a very different story.

Bonelli's eagle did not show up, and we returned empty-handed.

On the road back, on the western edge of the sierra we found twenty-odd griffons, looking like big bears, round a dead horse. The light was too bad to see much, but I am determined to attack them from a hide to-morrow.

APRIL 13TH. Up and about at 6 a.m. Made for the carcass at top speed. On the way we stopped to look at a calandra lark which was sitting up perkily on a small knoll. This is a very large species of lark with pronounced black marks on the throat, so well defined in this specimen that they seemed to stretch right across the throat and form a black bib. Actually it is broken in the middle like a Kentish plover's.

The griffons were busy at their grisly feast. Their numbers had swollen overnight, and they were now at least forty strong. There was a pariah dog at the carcass when we arrived and the cowardly vultures were standing impatiently round watching the interloper with restless displeasure. When we approached they were very slow to leave. Most just hopped away to a safe distance. Some retired on to the rocks behind; some even perched rather precariously, on a near-by pine.

I put up a quick hide and got inside, while T. and P. went off into the sierra to renew the search for Bonelli's eagle. Ten minutes sufficed to remove the scavenger's fears—or re-whet their appetites—and at last one bird risked it, and flew down close to

PLATE 8. MONTAGU'S HARRIER (FEMALE)

PLATE 9. THE "PARK" COUNTRY AT THE COTO DONANA

The big tree in the foreground held a Booted Eagle's nest. Black and Red Kites, Buzzards and Spanish Green Woodpeckers also nested here. In the undergrowth Dartford Warblers and Great Spotted Cuckoos were the most characteristic species

PLATE 10. PINE WOODS NEAR CORIA DEL RIO

Extensive pine woods of this type stretch away to the west of Coria. Raptors, particularly Black Kites, are conspicuous in this habitat

the carcass. Immediately the fun started. Great griffons piled in from all sides, not a few alighting right on top of their fellows. They quarrelled and fought over the offal with much feeling and evil greed. An impatient bird on the fringe would make a desperate attempt to get into the middle of things by leaping on top of the seething mass and fighting his way in to the corpse. Another, successful in securing a yard or two of entrail, came charging out of the mêlée and played tug-o'-war with a less fortunate rival at the other end. All the time there was a continuous hissing and grunting from the scrum. A number, apparently full fed, were standing idly by, taking no part in the foul feast. A stream ran close by and often the feeding birds ran to it for a drink. I could well imagine they needed it.

In the middle of this exhibition of filthy gluttony the pariah dog came back, this time with a mate. The griffons were immediately routed. So, nearly, was I, for they chose the rocks round my hide for perches while the dogs had their say in the matter. Some were as near as five yards, perched on low boulders, and as my hide was not unlike a rock, I began to have qualms lest one would choose it for his temporary resting place. The huge birds were so close that their baleful stare seemed to cut into my very skin. I began to appreciate the agonies of having broken a leg up there in the wild sierras and to imagine that these were the loathsome scavengers come to clean me up. Ugh!

I began to curse the dogs—beneath my breath, for I was a deal more frightened of them than I was of my vulture companions, some of which by now were almost within touching distance of the hide. The pariahs looked as though biting strangers was their regular pastime—to judge, at least, by their angry growls and the savage way they chased off any bold griffon who ventured from his ringside seat nearer to the carcass. By this time the entrails were all gone, and the ribs stuck up eerily. To my disgust I watched one of the dogs vanish entirely into the cavity of the horse! It reappeared all blood and filth. I was grateful that the hour was only 9 a.m. and not the heat of midday.

At the end of an hour the dogs departed. A second invasion of vultures began. This time the first birds to arrive on the scene tried to hold their priority of place by obstructing later arrivals

C
[33]

with full wing span—a fine sight. Not that it availed aught. They were simply jostled out of place. The bestial feast went on.

By now I had got through most of my photography, and I settled down to watch the birds. I was at once struck by the variations in colour between individuals. Some were very dark on the back, others light brown. One huge bird was almost buff on the scapulars. The normal extent of variation seemed to me to correspond closely with that which I have noticed in the great skua. The naked neck, too, differs. This on the ground is, of course, carried at its full serpentine length, and it is this which makes the griffon so gruesome to behold. In some it was just plain dirty white; in others slate blue. I was much amused, too, at their very deliberate goose-step walk.

At midday I could stand the stench no longer. When I got out, pandemonium reigned among the vultures. They stampeded in all directions. Rising from the ground is, for so heavy a bird, a laborious proceeding, for a long taxi is called for before they get under way, but once they are clear, they rise with superb ease. The great pinions are given a few flaps and, using the initial impetus thus gained, the bird rises without further flapping in ever widening spirals until it becomes a mere speck in the sky. On the ground the griffon may be ungainly and noisome, but in the air he is magnificent. Despite the feast I have just witnessed, the griffon remains for me a superb bird.

T. and P. eventually returned to the car. They had seen Bonelli—in the distance. We set out for the marsh which forms the estuary of the Barbate river. This is an extensive area of low country, much of it hard-baked mud liberally grown with *Salicornia*.

We stopped for lunch at its northern end. It is time that this diary recorded a few of my protests about Spanish food. This, even when hot, is to my stomach repulsive. When cold for picnic purposes, it defies description. To-day's menu contained cold omelette and fish (? species). It may not sound too bad, but when wrapped up in brown paper and oozing oil . . . well, I prefer starvation. Fortunately, food does not worry me much, and I am rapidly developing the technique of living on dry bread and oranges.

Near our parking place a vast concourse of buff-backed herons were feeding round a herd of swine in a particularly attractive setting of water and low trees. We have now seen buff-backs in frequent association with cattle, horses, and pigs, but not yet sheep. Perhaps they do not like them.

As soon as we got on to the arid areas, short-toed larks began to appear. Although, like all the larks, they do not wear an identity disc round their necks, these are nevertheless not difficult to identify. It is a lark in which the brown markings are less contrasted than in our species, and the general colour is very pale and washed out. Again, on the side of the neck are two darkish feather patches. These, however, are not very conspicuous in some specimens, and it requires a close view for their successful observation. I liked its song flight—high in the sky, but not the typical spiral of the skylark. Instead the bird dips upwards and downwards as it pours out its notes.

The marsh produced for me two more new species—avocet and little egret. Avocets need no description. They identify themselves, but the beauty of their black and white plumage, the elegance of those pale blue legs as they wade, and the curiosity of their tip-tilted bills, combine to make the first sight of them a notable event in the history of a bird watcher.

Much the same holds good for the little egret. To see those southern herons is the main object of my visit to Andalucia. At first glance it looked very like the buff-backs we have been seeing daily, for these have not even yet got the plumes from which they get their name. But this little egret on closer inspection was seen to have a slimmer and black bill. Its legs, too, are black, and when it rose from the water, its pale yellow feet were noticeable. Outlined against the blue sky it was an object of singular beauty.

On Barbate marsh were also numerous marsh and Montagu harriers, many blue-headed wagtails of the Spanish form, a few redshank, and a large flock of curlew.

We made our way back to Vejer, rapidly packed and sped down the eucalyptus-lined roads to Jerez, home of sherry. En route, in the pans of the salt mines near Cadiz, I saw my first black-winged stilts.

If the avocet is an elegant bird and one which by reason of its black and white patterning fascinates, the stilt even so goes one better, for not only has it the same attractive pied plumage, but in addition the curiosity of its huge red legs. Seen dead in a museum or in a painting—which till to-day was the only way I knew the stilt—it seems an ungainly freak, but wading in the shallows, it moves with an elegance beyond words to describe. In the air, too, it is almost equally fascinating, with its long legs stretched far behind the black wings and white body.

Jerez I shall remember for a number of things. Firstly, for the camel which I saw parked in a garage like a car—which made me laugh; secondly, for a good square meal, of which I was in dire need; thirdly for a bath of which the necessity was of even greater priority; and lastly for the heavenly smell of its orange trees in the dusk which, when I was washed and fed, made me feel life was indeed good. Nor must I forget our trip this evening to San Lucar de Barrameda. To-morrow we are off to the *marismas* of the Guadalquiver, the high spot of our trip. This evening we got into touch with Louis Bolero who is going to take us up the great river to the point where we can get horses to carry us into the delta. He is a cheerful Galician, far more dynamic than these sleepy Andalucians. Hearing of my inability to get any tobacco which did not burn like hay, he invited us to come down to Bonanza where by pulling the necessary customs wires he said he could get me some English stuff. T. decided on a bath, so P. and I went off in the car. We found Bolero in a pub with twelve other friendly gentlemen, sitting at a sort of King Arthur's Round Table. They were drinking cognac, so we joined in, but after fifteen 'rounds' I began to lapse into pleasant somnolence. Thank goodness P. was driving. As I write, the morning after, I am still without my tobacco.

APRIL 14TH. We left Bonanza at 10 a.m. On board Bolero's launch were, beside ourselves, two of his Spanish pals of the night before. They were still drinking—sherry this time, and there were bottles all over the boat! They had also brought a gun with them, and proceeded to outrage our feelings by taking pot shots at little terns which were diving for food round the boat. If the sherry fortunately disturbed their aims, it also equally unfortunately disturbed their ideas of security. After each battue the gun was put down, loaded and cocked, with the muzzle

snuggling against T's or my bottom. I kept repeatedly on the
move, with some justice.

The Guadalquiver is a fine, broad but muddy river. On the far
bank the ground was sandy and thickly grown with pines, over
which many black kites were wheeling. Up the river we saw grey
plover, redshank, bar-tailed godwit, dunlin, stilt, teal, little egret,
black-headed gull, mallard, whiskered tern, common heron, and
a raven.

Eventually the pines on the western shore died away and a
wilderness of arid mud-flat stretched away into mirage. Some
eight miles up the river we landed at a point previously arranged.
Here our horses and a guide were assembled, and in due course
we were ashore.

The *marismas* defy description. For what can pen write of a
wilderness whose dreary level runs away over miles of dried
cracked mud, with occasional lagoons formed from the rapidly
evaporating remnants of winter's floods? Dead dry sedges
sparsely cover the ground, and in the drier places scattered
patches of *Salicornia* provide the only vegetation that lives. All
around is mirage, water and trees and cattle, where in reality is
desert and waste and nothing. And over all the sun blazes from a
sky wherein no cloud disputes its mastery.

This grim land is our Mecca, as it has been for many other
ornithologists, and I have rarely been more excited than when
we set forth to-day. The *marismas* at last! 'Beyond the outer
fringes of the known world.' Even if Abel Chapman did feel that
such a description was a little too dramatic, I get the impression
of leaving behind the ordinary ways of life and arriving into
more primitive civilization. But primarily my excitement is due
to those who opened up the bird wonders of this strange corner
of Europe—and in particular, Abel Chapman; for it is essen-
tially *his* land. *Wild Spain* is an epic of bird and sporting literature. To read it, as I have read it in the past, sitting in an arm-
chair by the fire, is exciting enough. Little wonder that to turn
its pages here on the spot is to feel that one has at least achieved
one ambition of childhood days.

The *marismas*, and over there beyond the mirage, the Coto
Doñana! So long have those two been names, sacred names
almost that seemed distant, belonging to another world wherein

only the more fortunate ever in actual fact set foot. Yet here am I to-night sleeping at Las Nuevas, in the one house in the middle of this famous bird paradise. Dull indeed would he be who did not feel the echo of some thrill pass through him. And indeed our first taste of it to-day has not been without promise of what is yet to come.

As our horses plodded slowly forward we began to see birds. In the dry sedge growth we recorded the inevitable harriers, fan-tail warblers, calandra, and short-toed larks and Spanish yellow wagtails. By the first pool of water in this arid waste were countless birds—chiefly waders and terns—dunlin, sanderling, redshank, avocet, ringed and Kentish plovers. Of these the last was to me a new species, and an easy one to identify, too. His legs are black, his 'ring' is broken on the breast, and both above and below he is lighter in tone than the ring plover.

Here too were more whiskered terns, but also two more new species for me! Truly Spain is a little embarrassing for an ornithologist's first European bird trip. A few gull-billed terns appeared, but they were far off, and I had to accept T.'s identification rather than satisfy myself. A solitary Caspian tern, however, was an unexpected surprise. Its large size, as it squatted amongst the others, immediately attracted attention—a noble bird with bill of deepest coral red and rather a dark grey back.

By now we were nearing our first base—the *palacio* de Las Nuevas, a solitary shooting lodge, whitewashed as usual, and surrounded with a hedge of prickly pear. We dismounted, unpacked our food and stores, had lunch, and immediately in tropical heat set forth again. Our guide had told us where the flamingoes had been feeding that morning.

In a host of bird memories I can think of nothing so inspiring, so exciting, so beautiful as the experience we have had to-day. My mind conjures up many treasured memories, of my first black-throated divers in the wild setting of a Sutherland loch, of fulmars patrolling the sheer crags of Caithness cliffs, and of little red-necked phalaropes on a remote Shetland islet. But never have I been so moved by the sheer wondrous beauty of a bird as I was to-day by these flamingoes. To most men, it is said, there comes at least once a flash of the vision glorious. I feel that for me it has already shone forth.

[38]

We first saw the birds as a long thin pink line through the mirage. As we came closer, they assumed more definite shape. When wading through the shallows, the flamingoes' general colour scheme is a very soft pink. The body appears like a round ball precariously balanced on two long pink stilts. The long thin serpentine neck with the curious heavy downward-tilted bill completes a strange picture. When the bird feeds, it presents an odd doubled-up appearance, and as the long neck churns up with its beak the mud at its feet, it looks like a round, headless body mounted on three legs! Its wading is wondrous elegant. The legs are lifted high and clear of the water and each step is taken slowly and deliberately, as if to hurry would be undignified. The soft reflections of the long thin pale-pink line in water that took its colour from the blue of the sky defeat my poor pen for description.

Yet if the mere bird at rest leaves me without words, what am I to say of it in flight? Lovely as is the flamingo as it wades, it is a flash of glory when on the wing, for then instead of the soft pinks which predominate on the ground the bird exposes the brilliant scarlet of the covert feathers, scarlet that ends in the quill feathers of the primaries and secondaries in a marginal line of black. Nor was it just one bird in the air. Numbers on such a scale are difficult to estimate, but I do not think 1,500 far short of the birds that were here present.

When we had finished glorying in their beauty, we flushed them from the lagoon—a sight beyond belief. The blue sky was upon a sudden filled with countless scarlet birds, and in thronging mass they came back straight over our heads, clamouring, for all the world like geese. I vainly 'shot' them with my camera, but a monochrome photograph will never do justice to such wonders.

When the flamingoes had gone, we realized that the lagoon was thronged with many other birds. Stilt, redshank, dunlin, black-tailed godwit, greenshank, little stint, curlew-sandpiper (already slightly coloured), ring and Kentish plovers, avocet, lapwing, golden plover, pratincole, black and whiskered terns, widgeon, the inevitable Montagu, black kite (flying over), black-headed gull, spoonbill—twenty species, almost without moving! I settled down to take careful stock of those which were either new to me or interested me most. To take in all was impossible.

Black and whiskered terns were flying close past me along the line of the lagoon edge. It was a good opportunity to compare these two allied marsh terns. I came away with my earlier impressions from La Janda reinforced. Quite apart from the whiskered's white cheeks, the black tern *looks* black in flight, the whiskered merely dark grey. The latter's wings, too, are much lighter in colour.

Next the pratincoles held my attention. Here the glasses revealed a strange bird. In the air they are tern-like—an impression created by their long wings and pointed tail. On the ground they reminded me of diminutive Arctic skuas. The buff throat with its dark black streak on either side, and the rather sunken eye give it a strange dreamy look. This is certainly not a bird with which confusion is likely. It seemed more reptilian than avian.

The spoonbill describes itself. It was standing solitary and alone in the lagoon. I took it for an egret at first glance, for I saw only a white heron with black legs. But the spatulate bill with yellow tip gave it away, and I much admired the rich buff patch on its upper breast. It was inactive and did but little, content to rest on one leg with the other tucked away.

In the evening, back at the *palacio*, we pottered round the cactus hedge. It produced a cock woodchat, a white wagtail, and an ortolan bunting.

APRIL 15TH. To-day has been one of the most remarkable days I have ever spent after birds. We started by a brief inspection of the *palacio's* cactus bushes. These held a subalpine warbler, the white moustachial streak of which immediately attracted attention, another woodchat, a redstart, and a wryneck, shot by the boy of the house with a catapult. During this brief reconnaissance the flamingoes' serried ranks again passed over. How odd the flamingo looks in the air! His long neck stretches out in front of his body as far as his straggling legs protrude behind.

We packed up, mounted our sluggish horses and made over the *marismas* to the Coto Doñana, to the *palacio* from which Abel Chapman had done so much of his work. But much was to happen before ever we reached the Coto.

We called in first at the lagoon of the flamingoes. Here an even greater store of bird life awaited us than yesterday, although the flamingoes had departed. Mostly they were of the same species but greatly swollen in numbers, particularly the pratincoles which were buzzing about in all directions. A ruff was the only new wader, but the ranks of the black and whiskered terns had been swollen by many gull-billed terns. These last I could now watch in detail. They are most un-tern-like terns, midway, as it were, between these and the gulls, for they are heavily built and thick set. Their jet black heads and heavy black bills call to mind the Sandwich tern, but they have no long streamers for a tail. The most exciting addition to the bag was the slender-billed gull, of which there were three. Unfortunately, heat haze interfered badly with our views, but the telescope revealed it as a gull of the black-headed type, but with a long, thin, red bill, and with a white, not sooty brown head, and softly suffused with pink beneath.

The long ride across the open *marismas* from Las Nuevas to the Coto was remarkable chiefly for its heat and its mirage. The latter painted some remarkable pictures. Of birds the most noteworthy was the Marisma lark, which is of the short-toed type but with very distinctly defined dark markings on the upper breast.[1] They were frequenting the little knolls of ground two feet or so above the general flat level of this desert, hard-baked and cracked and plentifully studded with much dwarfed *Salicornia* scrub.

It was just after the episode of the larks that I saw some fast-moving shapes away to the left. I thought first of all it was mirage, then bulls. Finally they took definite shape and were camels. This is the famous wild herd of the Guadalquiver. Of its history I am in some doubt. I believe they were introduced for transport about a hundred years ago, but that, failing to serve their original purpose, they were turned loose, and have flourished in a wild state ever since. There were seven adults and one youngster, about half grown.

In time the barren *marisma* began to give place to a new country. Towards the sea high sandhills met the blue sky, here

[1] Because I have compared the Marisma lark with the short-toed lark, it must not be imagined that it is a sub-species of the latter. The short-toed is a separate species (*Calandrella brachydactyla*). The Marisma lark is a sub-species of *Calandrella rufescens*.

and there studded with pines, the source of whose nourishment made me wonder. Some were clearly buried up to half their trunks. Further to the west the ground was becoming less arid. Scrub and scattered tree growth appeared and a large house, the *palacio*, loomed up in uncertain outline out of the haze.

In another hour we were outside this, our new headquarters, and soon we were at work.

The true Coto Doñana is the sand-dune country to the south, with its scattered pine clumps. North and east it changes greatly. The whole ground is covered with thick bushes about thigh high. Amongst these grow clumps of pines, and scattered cork oaks of unusual size. Clumps of tamarisks show the edges of the many small lagoons. The whole area resembles a fine natural, but rather unkempt, park.

Into this we sallied forth. Almost immediately we were rewarded. On a fence post sat a great spotted cuckoo—a most distinguished bird, and not a bit like our own. Apart from the pronounced white spots on the wings, the bird is adorned with a well-defined crest and an unusually long tail. In flight, which is undulating, the long tail immediately attracts attention, and the contrast between the dark brown head and the buff neck and throat give a black and white appearance. Before our return to the *palacio* we had seen a number of them, and very noisy they were as they chased one another with rasping cries.

We eventually emerged on to a large lagoon, set in the midst of the low bushes and tamarisks. Its waters were without exaggeration black with ducks, while its shallow edges were seething with waders. T. rightly summed up the situation, 'You know, this is just indecent.' We settled down to inspect, and here is a mere list of species: ruddy shelduck, pintail, mallard, widgeon, teal, shoveler, garganey, gadwall, tufted duck, pochard, red-crested pochard, white-headed duck, spoonbill, flamingo, buff-backed heron, egret, black-necked grebe, dabchick and coot—those on the water, in a dense mass, in which it was impossible to feel that all the species had been detected. By the edges were spotted redshank, redshank, black-tailed godwit, common and wood sandpipers, stilt and avocet—again in great numbers, especially the last two.

I think I may be excused if I felt a trifle embarrassed by such wealth. But when my eyes had vainly tried to take in the magnificence of this scene, I found three species on which I wanted to concentrate. Except in a captive state I have not before seen the ruddy shelduck. I liked the unusual orange brown which is the predominant feature of their colour scheme. Their light-coloured heads look rather odd, but the black wings and tail show up well. In the red-crested pochard the head of the drake is a fine rich golden brown, but I liked especially the contrast between the bold black breast and underparts which in flight clash sharply with the white patches on the flanks. The white-headed duck is on the other hand rather ludicrous. As its name implies, it has a white head, but its characteristic is its long pheasant-like tail, which is normally carried level with the water, but from time to time is cocked up in a sharp point—an absurd gesture.

When I went to bed to-night, a grand moon was lighting up the Coto, and it is with the eerie crying of the stone curlews we have not yet seen that I lay down my pen.

APRIL 16TH. I went down to the lagoon of many fowl this morning with a hide and camera in the hope that I might get some photographs of stilts wading. I had no little difficulty in locating it in this unending flat expanse, over which it is impossible to get a bird's eye view. Although the birds were so numerous, they had an uncanny habit of keeping just out of range of my lenses, and I spend a fruitless morning, though I exposed a few plates at extreme distance. By midday the heat was colossal, and in my tent I all but expired. Unable to stand it any longer, I emerged and dragged my hot tired body back to the *palacio* where I spent half an hour stretched out naked on the bed.

Refreshed, I sallied forth again—clothed, of course! T. and P. had gone off to look for imperial eagle and were not due back till 2 p.m. Our stores had now dwindled to nothing but a bit of dry bread and a very few oranges, so that lunch was out of the question. Having an hour to spare, I took a stroll to the north of the *palacio* where many scattered cork oaks created an attractive park. Immediately I found two pairs of white storks nesting, Their huge piles of sticks were sited right on top of two cork oaks and for a while I sat down and watched their red-billed, red-legged occupants. Resuming, I next flushed a buzzard from a

nest in a cork oak, and the bird went out *pee-oo-ing* in noisy
alarm. Soon I realized that I had walked straight into a colony
of black kites. Nests, old or in the course of construction, of
raptors—mostly I imagine black kites—were in nearly every tree.
I climbed to eight. None yet held eggs, but several were lined
with the paper and string which characterize the kite's architecture. Where they get their materials from in this wilderness
intrigues me! It is a fine thought—a wretched black kite scouring
the barren Coto in a desperate attempt to remain true to type by
finding the necessary string!

Then a red kite circled over and gave me a splendid chance to
compare the two allied species. In actual fact the two are easily
separable. In addition to the very much darker general colour
scheme, the black kite's tail is shorter and with very little fork in
it. In the red kite the colour scheme is altogether lighter. Near
the wing tips, just where the primaries begin on the underside
are conspicuous white patches, while the tail is notably long and
very markedly forked. The head too seems to be lighter.

The red kite was circling round in great spirals, and I began to
have hopes of a nest, but time was now getting on and I returned
to find T. and P. They had seen imperial eagle, in the distance at
least.

In the afternoon we got our horses and a guide to take us to
the famous 'white' heronries which are the great glory of the
Coto. It was indeed to see these *pajereras* that in particular I at
least had come to Andalucia. Memories of earlier reading from
Abel Chapman, and the photographs of Farren, Lodge, and
Beetham have always made a visit to this bird paradise one of
my most inspiring desires. The moment seemed now to have
come.

Our route apparently was to take us past my raptors' nests of
this morning. So I was playing the part of cicerone. When I got
to the two stork nests, I went through the correct procedure—or
so I believe—to stop my horse. The effect was astonishing. The
old chestnut tore the rope reins from my hands and bolted. Now
I am not an equestrian, but in the *marismas* it is a case of needs
must. Up to date the old nags we had mounted had been so
docile, even in the presence of camels, that even I had begun to
wish that they would show a little more enterprise. However, as

a means of locomotion they served their purpose. I had imagined therefore that the old chestnut on which I was now for the first time mounted would be as tractable as the rest. On that account I had, for all my ignorance of riding, taken but little notice of its lack of harness. It had rope for reins, a few sacks for a saddle and no stirrups. And the brute bolted me. The country being woodland, I was soon imagining my skull cracked open on a protruding branch. As it was, they whistled over my head, while I clung on by the beast's mane and tucked my head flat into its neck. I hung on like grim death, and to my relief after half a mile the beast stopped. I do not mind admitting that I dismounted quickly, before another wasp—or whatever it was—stung it in the backside. All the same, I am feeling rather pleased with myself for managing, no rider as I am, to stay on a bolting horse, on which there were no stirrups at all, practically no saddle, and the reins of which I had lost.

As we rode out, buff-backed herons began to get increasingly numerous, and as we found some comparatively tame cattle surrounded by them, I got out the camera and tried some shots. In due course we came to the heron nesting trees. That this was *a* breeding colony was obvious from the many hundreds of old stick nests that festooned the tamarisks, but it was equally obvious that it was not *the* colony. There was nothing here with which I could associate the mental pictures I had of these great breeding places from other writers. There was no real lagoon, to begin with, no background of sand dunes; nor was there evidence of the multitudes which I had been led to believe bred in the Coto. Truly there were many hundreds of old nests, whitewashed still from last year's breeding season. Even so, I am convinced that to-day we have not actually been to *the* spot. Yet the guide does not seem to know anywhere else. I am wondering if he is not just deliberately unwilling to take us to the right place. Perhaps he brews potheen—or the Spanish equivalent—there!

That the birds are not breeding here this year is clear, for they should now at least be starting nesting operations. It is very obvious that we have struck an unfortunately dry season. I gathered the same from our guide at Las Nuevas, and I seem to remember photographs of the *marismas* proper far more flooded than they are at the moment. All these birds are probably much affected by water level. However, nesting or not, there were myriads of birds round the place. Buff-backed herons were *everywhere*. On all sides flocks could be seen either dotted about the ground or in the air, flashing white dots against the ultramarine blue of the sky.

As evening drew in, they began to congregate near the apparently abandoned breeding haunt. They started coming in to roost in flocks of twenty or more. Each flock made for one or two trees, and before we left we actually *counted* up to 700 in two trees. We gave up figures after that, and they were still arriving when we left. The sight can be left to the imagination. The trees were just a white, squawking mass—a scene of surpassing loveliness.

Near the buff-backs—which by the way are beginning to assume their buff plumes on head, back, and breast—were a few night herons. This is a sinister-looking bird—an impression created by its black crown which in the settled bird is drawn right back into the mantle. Yet the general colour scheme is pleasing—soft greys on the throat and breast, darker grey on the wings, and blue-black on the back. Its stocky build is apparent both when settled and in flight. In the air, indeed, its stumpiness is exaggerated by the shortness of its tail.

APRIL 17TH. We have spent the whole day pottering about the scrub country near the *palacio* and particularly about my raptor trees. In my short three-quarters of an hour yesterday I had seen what an interesting bit of ground this was. So we decided to spend the morning at least in working it more thoroughly. Nor were we disappointed. We started by examining my buzzard of yesterday, and we put birds off two more eyries, to one of which I climbed. It held the usual clutch of three. I also climbed to several of the suspected black kites, and in one of them I found a single egg, so that laying evidently is just beginning. The egg was white in ground colour with a fairly generous sprinkling of brown and sepia spots and blotches.

Passing the black kite colony, we saw the red kite again, circling over the scattered cork oaks, and settled down to watch it. As we were doing this we noticed a Sharpe's green woodpecker busily excavating a hole in a tree—about five feet from the ground. At least I infer it was of this sub-species, but I could not make out through the glasses the small differences which separate this race from our own. At the same time, to my amazement, a pair of mounted civil guards came riding past. To my greater amazement they took no notice of us. If, as it seemed, we were such objects of suspicion elsewhere in Andalucia, it was not a little surprising that they should have ignored three obvious curiosities away out in this wilderness.

The red kite was still in the air. It seemed so attached to a certain area that we thought a search for a possible nest was indicated. Nor had we to look far, and soon we had flushed its mate from a bulky stick nest high up a cork oak. I again climbed, and this time the nest had its full clutch of three eggs. They were remarkably like buzzard's, and I was glad that we had seen an undoubted kite leave the nest. Actually the inevitable newspaper and string would have told of its owner's identity. The eggs varied, also, like buzzard's; one was well marked, another fairly so; the third was a very poor specimen with very faint spots.

We saw several hobbies as we came back—almost certainly migratory birds freshly arrived and moving north—and one big surprise, a lanner falcon, which I did not see as well as I should have liked. The impression I got was of a washed-out looking peregrine, streaked instead of barred.

We returned for 'lunch', if our now sadly reduced supply of very dry bread and oranges could be honoured by such a title. The food problem was really beginning to get serious, when suddenly the inmates of the *palacio* seemed to realize that we were not looking as full fed as we ought. Here at the *palacio* we feed along with 'the family' (sort of caretakers, I imagine) on a rickety wooden table, and here we have been eating—and conserving—our unappetizing provisions, while the family sit down to their feasts of eggs, etc.—all very tantalizing to empty stomachs.

I came in first and was getting out the last remaining loaf, when the good lady of the house asked me if we would like eggs! T. and P., I think, nearly fell on their knees. I recovered my presence of mind sufficiently to realize that Spanish eggs would probably be fried—and, if so, almost certainly in oil. I managed to convey that I wanted mine boiled, but the other two took theirs fried.

[47]

I think I won. Indeed, I know I did—for never have I seen anything so filthy as an egg fried in olive oil. T. confessed afterwards that had he not been *in extremis*, he could never have got through it.

This afternoon we got out the horses (I carefully avoided the chestnut), and pushed again into the raptor ground. So far we had really explored but very little of it, and that little had been so good that our conservatism can hardly be blamed. We had hopes of seeing our lanner again, and in the distant pines perhaps imperial eagle. We saw neither, but we did locate a pair of booted eagles, fine fellows, most conspicuously patterned on the under wing, which is far lighter than in any other raptor I know.

In due course I saw a large nest up a cork oak—an easy climb, even without the irons—and to my joy it was the occupied eyrie, for it held one large but uninspiring white egg. We spent half an hour or so watching the adult eagles circling round. How I wish I had the time to set about photographing this glorious creature!

Spain does nothing by halves. I had not seen a golden oriole, so this afternoon she, of her bounty, provided no less than three —all cocks. I cannot help feeling that I have been peculiarly fortunate in my introduction to this glorious bird. A bird of the tall tree tops, it is in such a setting difficult to see well, as I discovered in the case of the other two to-day. But this first bird was on the open bush country, and I could revel in the glory of its brilliant colours without the distraction of glittering foliage. Its yellows are beyond belief, so vivid that no comparisons can possibly serve to call home its brilliance. But it is the contrast of these flashing yellows with the jet black of the wings that is so striking. As it flew from bush to bush, it lit up the countryside like a rocket on Guy Fawkes' night. Not even in the flamingo is the colour scheme so flashingly brilliant.

We were now moving out into the bush country from the 'park' which held so many raptors. Watching birds from horseback is not a good method, and although for a while we tried it, for the high view point is a great advantage, we had to give it up —not before, however, T. had given us a good laugh. He had his glasses up to his eyes, and elbows accordingly bent. His horse was plodding slowly on. It took him under a tree where a side branch caught him under the elbows with his glasses still up!

PLATE 11. SALICORNIA ON THE OPEN MARISMA

On the skyline are the famous marisma camels, and in the far distance the trees round the *palacio* at the Coto Donana. Marisma Larks were particularly abundant in this area

PLATE 12. LAGUNA DEL TORERO

An off-shoot of La Janda. Crested Coots and Ferruginous Ducks were characteristic birds of the open water. The reed beds held Purple Gallinules, Marsh Harriers, Great Reed and Cetti's Warblers. The tamarisks were occupied by Buff-backed Herons

PLATE 13. BUFF-BACKED HERONS—MALE AND FEMALE ON GUARD

After that we walked. The immediate result was that I flushed a hen Dartford warbler from a nest which contained three newly hatched chicks.

I now left T. and P. to continue their exploration, while I turned my horse in the direction of the heronry we had visited yesterday, and here I spent an hour or so making exposures in flight of the buff-backs and night herons. Apart from them—and a few little egrets—I saw little that was new. I got excellent views of a black-eared wheat-ear, again of the light-throated variety, and I was particularly struck by the buff neck. It seemed more intense than it had been in the first bird I saw at La Janda.

APRIL 18TH. I woke this morning to the monotonous droning of a hoopoe in the trees outside my bedroom window. I dressed and sallied forth after him. I am beginning to run out of superlatives for the description of these brilliant coloured species. Bee-eater, roller, flamingo, oriole, and now hoopoe! All that one can say is that it is a huge tiger moth—pink brown in general colour with sharply contrasted black-and-white wings. Such a description leaves out of account its fine crest, pink, like the rest of the head and shoulders, but with black tips to each plume. It is normally carried closed, in which position it protrudes behind the crown, but on occasion it is fully expanded, particularly when the bird is alarmed or nervous.

To-day we have left the Coto and have settled in at Coria del Rio, just south of Seville, and at the north end of the *marismas*. The original plan was that I should stay behind in the Coto for a week or so and get on with some photography of the herons and the raptors. Indeed I had laboriously brought all my tree-hide stuff on horses across the delta. But the herons were not breeding, and the raptors only just starting business. Above all, the food problem was getting really acute. So here I am, still with the party, dearly though I should have liked to try that booted eagle.

It was a long ride from the *palacio* to Las Marismillas where we had arranged for Louis Bolero to pick us up again in his motor-boat. Nor was it particularly remarkable for its birds. The ride took us along the southern edge of the *marismas* and always in sight of the pine and sand-dune area. I shall remember it chiefly for

D   [49]

its tropical heat, which I felt all the more because I was wearing gum boots—rather foolish perhaps, but an attempt to get round the difficulties of packing. My feet rapidly became like slabs of roast beef, and I had eventually to ride in stockinged feet.

The ground here was slightly above the general level of the main *marisma*, and was consequently more hard-baked and liberally grown with *Salicornia*. It was an ideal sand grouse habitat. We were not therefore surprised to flush a pair—but they were far away, and it was impossible to see them at all adequately. Probably they were pin-tailed sand grouse.

After our long ride over the shadeless delta it was refreshing to turn the horses into the thickly pine-wooded area which for some miles here fringes the Guadalquiver. This was singularly attractive country, and I should greatly have liked to explore it further, but apart from the necessity of meeting Bolero, even if the spirit was willing, the flesh was very weak, perspiring and exhausted, a condition due not so much to the heat of the sun as to the lack of food we have experienced during these last few days.

We stopped at a glorious lodge in this pine country—Las Marismillas, with a stork's nest in the grounds. Here we unloaded the horses, paid off our guide, and got the paraphernalia aboard Bolero's boat. In the course of this job we alarmed a small flock of azure-winged magpies. As they flitted away through the wood, I got the impression of a cuckoo-like bird, with long tail and very rasping note. But as we were on our way to Coria, which is one of their main headquarters, I was content with this fleeting glimpse and pursued them no further. T. and P. did so, however, while I took a much needed siesta on the launch.

On the journey back to Bonanza we had a most unexpected sherry party. A friend of Bolero's, who had for a little worked in London, had come along 'to practise the English', and as a sort of fee to his long-suffering tutors had brought with him a case of sherry. Now liquid refreshment had not been the least of our trials in the Coto. We had quickly run out of all our wine, and had had to rely largely on oranges. Once only, in desperation, had we broken the rule of never drinking Spanish water. I need hardly say, therefore, that we viewed this new source with delight—but we were also very empty of stomach. Consequently, when we reached Bonanza . . .

We did our best to say good-bye to Bolero, ungaraged the car and drove a decidedly uncertain course to Jerez, where a good bath and a meal soon put us right.

Thence to Seville where we did some shopping, and in due course have landed here at Coria del Rio, where we are housed in a most peculiar little pub. We have had information that this pub is amongst the most lousy in Europe, so we are preparing for a lively night. The Spanish equivalent of Keatings was *not* forgotten amongst our purchases in Seville!

APRIL 19TH. I awoke with a start. I opened my eyes dreamily to see a most agile creature running about the bedroom wall a few inches from my face. It was striped in yellow and black, and in my drowsy state it loomed into my half-conscious mind like a tiger. I shot upright, whereupon with unhesitating speed it too shot into a hole in the rafters.

It was a fitting end to a most amusing night. As I noted yesterday, we had been warned about the Coria pub, and it certainly was not prepossessing, for it was a mere poverty-stricken house in a back street. We retired early last night and spent an hour with the Keatings. The wooden beds looked very suspicious; the mattresses looked a certainty. If one or other did not harbour bed bugs, then I just do not know their typical habitat at all.

We dealt suitably with the most likely lairs, and then turned to the wooden ceiling, in which the rafters were pitted with holes. More probable lairs! Impossible to deal with these. So we retired and, when the candles were out, lay back and waited for the first bite. Strangely enough it never came, but I spent a night of dreams all the same. Hence my sudden alarm, in my half-conscious state, at the apparition of the yellow-and-black striped monstrosity, upon which my bleary eyes first opened. It was, of course, only a gecko—an ally, in fact, for he too fights the bugs.

We emerged to find ourselves besieged by a herd of goats which the local milkman drove from door to door and 'tapped' according to the demands of his clients. Disentangling ourselves, we set about getting into touch with Miguelitto, who, we had been told, will act as our guide in this region.

Miguelitto is a character worthy of some comment. He is a real tough but a good-hearted Spaniard, dressed in blue dungarees and with knives in his belt. If I had met him in the sierras I should have without hesitation run a mile. But he knows his birds—the only Spaniard we have met who does so. For long he has acted as a guide to English egg-collectors in this part, and he knows his geese that lay their golden eggs. This was painfully obvious during to-day, for he has been clearly much perplexed and, I think, quite annoyed, because we did not loot the nests we found in his company, even though they were only buzzard and common kestrel. For all that he is invaluable to us.

We set off on horseback to the pinewood country to the west of Coria. The country here is flat, as one would expect, for it is the beginning of the Guadalquiver delta, but extensive tree growth stretches away to the north-west. We spent the day in these woods. Except for azure-winged magpies it has been our least profitable day. But we did see these beautiful magpies very well. They remind me in many ways of the great spotted cuckoos, due largely to their long tails and rasping notes. This long tail and the wings are azure, and their backs grey, ending in red-brown flanks—a really lovely combination.

In some tall pines we found a great colony of black kites. The nests were like a small rookery, and we counted eighteen birds at once in the air. In this same area we found also two nests of buzzard and two of common kestrel. The only new small bird we saw was crested tit—the south Spanish sub-species.

APRIL 20TH. A most exacting and exciting day, if not very productive. We have been into the Isla Menor after little bustard, but as I write, bulls rather than birds are the most vivid memory.

We had first to get the horses across the Guadalquiver, which was accomplished by means of a sort of canal barge. Then started a long and very tiring ride. I think these Coria horses are even worse than the Las Nuevas ones, if possible. I certainly tried every position, side saddle, lying flat, astride—but one was as bad as another. As a result, I walked most of the way. Not only was it more comfortable; it was also quicker.

PLATE 14. BUFF-BACKED HERONS—MALE AND FEMALE AT NEST

PLATE 15. BUFF-BACKED HERONS—MALE AND FEMALE CONSTRUCTING NEST

After a seemingly endless time over this dreary flat land we came at last to wide acres of monotonous pasture. According to Miguelitto, this was the terrain beloved of the little bustard. For myself I was chiefly aware that it was certainly beloved of fighting bulls. They were on all sides of us—huge-shouldered, magnificent beasts, the glory of the bull ring. They may adorn an arena, but they spoilt my day in the Isla Menor. Every now and then one would ponderously rise as the horses passed it and look nasty—very nasty indeed. One gentleman looked more than usually ugly, and even the placid Miguelitto advised care. Believe me, I needed no second admonishment! Next time I come here I am hiring a matador.

Looking for little bustard in such company was a joke. T. flushed one which gave him only a glimpse. It pitched in a rough field and we did our level best to get it up again, but without success. For the rest, I had one and three quarters of an eye on the bulls which did not leave me overmuch sight for bird watching.

Our one success was quite fortuitous. In the process of observing the suspicious antics of one of these gentlemen I did not feel my leisurely horse lower its head to feed, and consequently I went straight over its mane, to the consternation of a calandra lark which was sitting on a nest containing one egg. I should not wonder if she laid it out of sheer fright. The nest was sited like a skylark's but the egg was very different—large, as one would expect from this bird, and far less brown in its colour scheme. Indeed, its ground colour was bluish white.

I was not sorry when we left the bull areas behind and emerged on to ground covered with low scattered bushes. This is the breeding haunt of the black-bellied sand-grouse, and ere long we saw a pack of about ten. They are wild things and take a deal of seeing to advantage. We chased them about the flats, and after many short and usually unsatisfactory views I came away with the impression of a big golden plover, very black underneath, rather pinkish on top. In flight the wings are markedly sickle-shaped, and they carry the bird away at a rare pace. Later we saw several pairs of one other pack.

APRIL 21ST. Horses all day again! O for a bit of shanks pony!

Miguelitto had told us of a pair of Bonelli's eagles which he said regularly occupied an eyrie in a tall 'parasol' pine. As Bonelli usually breeds in the most fearsome crags, this seemed a good chance both to see the birds and to inspect the nest.

The long ride took us along sandy tracks through pine country of surpassing loveliness. It was an area of woodland which fascinated me and I would gladly have spent hours in it.

En route we had a stroke of luck. We found a rufous warbler which seemed to realize we were anxious to observe it, and instead of retiring into the undergrowth after the manner of its kind sat out in the open and displayed itself to us. No bird could have behaved better. As its name implies, the rufous warbler has rich red-brown as its dominant colour, but it is its lovely tail which is this fine bird's great glory. This is fan-shaped and a rich dark rufous (as also is the rump), and each feather—except, I think, the central ones—has a black and white margin. The tail is in constant motion and is flirted up and down and quite frequently carried high in a wren-like posture. Through the eye runs a dark streak with a well-defined light stripe above it.

In the Bonelli country we once again found black kites very numerous, as also were common kestrels. We noted two booted eagles and several buzzards, one of which we put off a nest. Of smaller birds hoopoes were much in evidence to-day. I saw my first chaffinch in Spain. A woodlark was heard singing; a short-toed tree creeper also.

When at last we came to Miguelitto's locality, Bonelli was not at home. We had a long hunt round about, but with no result. A pair of Egyptian vultures seemed peculiarly attached to a tree with a large nest in it. As this bird does sometimes use trees instead of crags, we had hopes that we would find them breeding —but like Bonelli it came to nothing.

APRIL 22ND. When we reached the garage this morning, we found the V.8 had serious engine trouble. Fortunately Fords are cars about which Spanish mechanics know something, so we left them to it, and in the meantime hired a real old bone-shaker which looked in imminent danger of collapse and with tyres through which the inner tube was showing. The garage hand seemed quite perplexed when we expostulated at their condition. Still, it was Hobson's choice, and into our new chariot we packed ourselves and Miguelitto. Even the prospect of numerous punctures was better than another day in the saddle.

We have been into the Isla Mayor after great bustard and pin-tailed sandgrouse. This is not unlike the Isla Menor but is more cultivated, and, thanks be, with a much reduced population of bulls. Under Miguelitto's direction we searched many areas for bustard but without success. At last in a huge bean field we found them. We first put up a large pack of eight, later a pair, and afterwards an odd bird or so. They are exceeding wary creatures, and on no account admit of a close approach. In the bean fields the birds keep so low that despite their great size they are very difficult to see. Indeed all day we have not had a good view of the standing bird.

In flight I had not visualized them as such huge birds. They were of the size of turkeys on the wing. Seen thus, they show a lot of white, for the wings, although dark in the quills and scapulars, have a broad white patch in the middle. We spent a long time on this ground trying to re-locate the birds we had flushed, but they had travelled far and we did not see them again. As we returned to the car, there were many griffons and one Egyptian vulture circling over a field. There was probably a carcass, but we did not inspect.

Thence to the ground where the pin-tailed sandgrouse nest. This much resembles that on which we found the black-bellied two days ago—hard-baked mud with sandy patches and grown, at frequent intervals, with low tufts of *Salicornia*. It is to be noted that both *ganga* and *corteza*—to give them their attractive Spanish names—like semi-bushy country of this nature adjoining open grassland. I noticed too that while the black-bellied seemed to keep to the edge of the bushes and were reluctant to pitch in the scrub, the pin-tailed had a decided preference for the protection of the bushy ground, and when flushed on the edge made straight for it.

Of the birds themselves we caught glimpses of about a dozen, but they were appallingly wild, more so even than the black-bellied, if that is possible. From what little I saw of them the only

[55]

feature which struck my attention was the pin-tailed's slimmer build. The one is a big, heavy bird; the other a trimmer, neater fellow altogether.

Marisma larks were much in evidence on this ground.

It was while we were after the sandgrouse that it had the nerve to rain. After an unbroken period of scorching sun we got a shower—and a heavy one. It did not worry us much, but poor Miguelitto's summer suiting of thin dungarees was not tailored for such inclement weather, and when it was over and he stood up from the shelter of a low bank, he looked very comical and but half himself with his garments clinging pitiably about him.

To-morrow we leave here. Our next destination has been in some doubt, for T. has only another three days before he has to catch a train at Seville. Far afield is out of the question. We have decided to return to Vejer, for there is much of La Janda which we have not yet seen. And if that fails, there is Cape Trafalgar where ospreys are reputed to nest.

APRIL 23RD. From Coria back to Vejer via Seville and Jerez. I am not sorry to have left Coria. It is a dirty little town and the distances to the bird grounds are considerable, the country dull and lifeless—with the exception of the bulls!—and the bird life not so thick as elsewhere. I am getting spoilt; that is obvious!

In point of fact, the move has turned out to be peculiarly fortunate. But let events be told in their order.

As we neared Vejer, buff-backed herons grew ever-increasingly numerous. Such a feature of the landscape had they now become that before ever we had arrived we were discussing the possibility of a breeding colony somewhere on La Janda. The only other explanation was that they were birds which, finding the *marismas* dry, were reconciled to a non-breeding year. But if so, why were they congregating here, so obviously at Vejer? We were to have the answer sooner than we knew.

We arrived at lunch time, parked our things in the old pub, found the old crowd of sombrero-hatted, cylindrical-trousered, silent gentlemen to see us arrive and depart, and took our lunch down to the bridge. Here the river curves in a wide sweep, first west and then, by many meanders, due east into La Janda. This valley runs round a large rocky hill where is sited the cottage in which, I believe, Willoughby Verner lived.[1]

We stopped just beyond this hill along the eucalyptus-lined road and lunched in the pleasant shade of an ilex, where a cirl bunting, the first we had noted, sang to us. We followed a tiny stream through the cork oaks and wild olives until we came to a tributary of the Barbate which clearly marked the beginning of La Janda. This followed the edge of the slight hillside, so we in turn followed its course. It produced the loud blast which signifies the presence of Cetti's warbler, but as usual the bird remained an enigma. While T. and P. were examining this ground, I pottered up a low spur which jutted out into the flat marshes to examine a few of the large nests I could see in the pines. But when I reached the top, it was not the old raptors' nests that called my attention, for beyond, where the lagoon again twisted in beyond my spur, was a sight for tired eyes—hundreds of white herons in trees, reeds and the neighbouring fields. So this is the explanation of our suspicions. And we are not to return home, despite our failure in the *marismas*, without seeing the white heronries which are the great glory of Andalucian bird life.

We were not long in getting round to the centre of activities, and then what a sight! Every sallow tree—and they were only big bushes—was *festooned* with stick nests. I counted one hundred and eight in one small corner that was a mere iota of the whole! The branches were thronged with white birds, squawking, fighting, building, alighting, departing. A constant stream kept coming and going in unbroken succession. In the reed bed a mere clap of the hands flushed a locust storm of buff-backs.

Numbers in such circumstances must always be suspect. I can only feebly mutter that there were thousands. Two thousand pairs would, I think, about fit the bill, but actual figures mean little. The reality is magnificent. It has not inspired me as the flamingo did, but it has thrilled me to the core, the more so because it is so unexpected. For in its thronging life, its animation, its baffling variety of incident it can only be compared to a sea-bird colony. Indeed it is a little overwhelming, and words cannot possibly do justice to its wonder. The breeding trees were

[1] Author of *My Life among the Wild Birds in Spain.*

in a small semi-circle, no more than a hundred yards across, and standing in the middle we were almost entirely surrounded by buff-backs. Behind over the spur white Vejer glistened in the blazing sun.

Temporarily sated and overpowered by the scene, we inspected individuals. They were nearly all buff-backs, and now at last this name rang true. In the last ten days their plumes have been assumed with astonishing speed, for they are now buff on crown, back, and breast. It is a very rapid transformation. Amongst them were a few little egrets. One I saw on a nest; but egrets are but an infinitesimal portion of the colony.

I inspected a number of nests, but only one contained an egg, and that a singleton. The nests are very flimsy stick constructions, cupless yet with the twigs round the edges carefully built up above the general level, doubtless to give protection to the eggs. Most of the birds are building, and both sexes help in this task as I saw in the case of several pairs.

To-day I have only examined the nests in the sallows which I could reach from dry land, but I am much intrigued by the activity in the reed bed. As it contains twice as many birds as the trees I am certain that they are breeding there too—but the water is deep, and I had no thigh waders this afternoon.

From the information we have it seems clear that this is a new and unrecorded colony, for we have only heard of those in the *marismas* before.[1] Yet it is certainly not of this year's foundation, for some of the nests are obviously of at least last season's construction.

When we had recovered from this unexpected stroke of luck, we turned our attention to the open water of the lagoon round the buff-backs' nesting trees. Here were a score or so of ferruginous ducks. I thought they looked very like more richly coloured tufted females. Although at a little distance rather dull of appearance, a close view through the glasses shows a very jolly bird. Ferruginous suits well for a name, for russet red is the predominant colour of the upper parts of the drake, especially rich on the head. My first impressions were of a rather dull bird, but the more I watched them, the more fascinating I found the unusual richness of their at first sight drab colour scheme. I liked,

[1] Mr. W. H. Riddell has since also recorded a colony near Arcos.

too, the saucy, white eye which stood out like a bead in the russet head.

Afloat and awing the ferruginous duck presents two entirely different colour schemes, for while on the water it is dark and drab, in the air conspicuous whites appear as it were from nowhere, particularly on the wings. Few of the 'dark' ducks, i.e. those which are not light coloured in their general make-up like shelduck or smew, show so much white. In fact I liked the ferruginous drake very much.

With them were also many mallard, quite a few coot, and an odd waterhen, whilst marsh harriers constantly drifted over the reed beds, in which great reed warblers churned out their harsh songs. I could see but little of these fellows, but their size is markedly bigger than that of our own bird.

On the way back through the wild olives and cork oaks I had some excellent views of more orphean warblers. My first impressions were confirmed. I again noted the way the black brown runs down as a dark mat and merges gradually into the dull grey-brown of the back.

APRIL 24TH. We have spent the day at the Laguna del Torero— as, if I read my map aright, our *pajerera* is called. I spent the morning in a hide on one of the lower tree-nesting buff-backs. The nest contained only one egg, so that the bird spent most of the time on simple sentry duty. Nevertheless, incubation clearly begins at least spasmodically with the laying of the first of the clutch, for the bird this morning spent quite a few periods in sitting.

Later I spent a grand hour or two inspecting the reed bed. As I surmised yesterday, this indeed holds much of the colony. The birds were in clouds, and as I first stepped in they rose in a white, squawking, protesting mass. Loosely built nests of dried rushes liberally adorned every little clump of reeds. I counted no less than eight nests in one small tuft. Such sites, which would befit purple herons, are apparently uncommon. The *Practical Handbook*, our only reference, says that they are unusual. Yet here more than half the colony has adopted the reeds instead of the trees for breeding purposes.

Laying is only just beginning. I saw many nests containing one egg, and only one with two.

I lingered a long while in this paradise, surrounded by a never-dwindling cloud of buff-backs, glistening angelic white against the bright blue sky. The scene fascinated; I felt I wanted to cling on, just standing there feasting my eyes, watching these lovely white herons in their many activities, for they are ridiculously tame and soon recover from the shock of disturbance.

I next turned to the open lagoon, and there watched in turn little egret and night heron, for a flock of these last had now occupied a single sallow growing out of the deeper water. It was instructive to have buff-back and egret in the field of the glasses at the same time.

Now that full plumage has been adorned the two species differ widely. The buff plumes of the one on crown, breast, and back are as delicate as those of the other, but their very colour readily identifies the birds. The egret's plumes indeed are so fine that unless they are erected, they are almost invisible as they lie down the bird's back. In addition, the egret's legs are black and its feet a bilious yellow, the buff-back's a garish puce pink; the bill, in the one black, is in the other yellow-tipped shading into red at the base—though the intensity of these colours varies considerably with individuals. Again, the egret has a sinister yellow eye, which in the buff-back is bright pink. But it is in general carriage that they differ most. The egret's long, thin neck, even when drawn into its back, gives it a slimmer build than its more bull-necked cousin.

If the egret has a sinister glance, its snowy white plumes more than correct that first unfortunate impression, but the night heron has no such saving grace. Very stockily built, robed in dark attire, it looks the embodiment of an evil spirit, as, perched upon a branch, it twists its sinuous neck around to observe the intruder. Yet it too on a close inspection has its points, for it is a beautiful combination of greys and blue-blacks, and the long cream plumes which sprout from the crown add a touch of light to this bird of the night. Its eye, too, is a vivid and penetrating crimson, of great depth. The legs were very noticeably bright pink.

P. then came up and said that the majority of the coot we had yesterday noted as belonging to the common species were in reality crested coot! In some surprise I turned the glasses on the

PLATE 16. BUFF-BACKED HERON—TREE SITE

PLATE 17. BUFF-BACKED HERON—TREE SITE

PLATE 19

PLATE 18

swimming birds, and after careful scrutiny I saw that he was right. For the tops of their bald pates were indeed adorned with small red lobes. It might be thought that these would be readily conspicuous. It is not the case. On the contrary, only when the bird is close can they be seen at all clearly. Afar they merge into the black plumage. Obviously on ground where both species occur *all* coot must be subjected to the closest scrutiny.

I now hid up for an hour or so in a thick bush and waited for things to happen on the lagoon. My old friends, the ferruginous ducks, soon reappeared, and I got some excellent close views. The white eye is *most* characteristic when the bird is near, but out on the lake the white under-tail coverts alone help identification. The half-dozen or so birds were all drakes. At last out of the reeds came a duck, and, to my joy, accompanied by a brood of seven ducklings. This is undoubtedly remarkably early, for the authorities give the beginning of May as the start of the nesting season, and the incubation period as twenty-five days. This would bring the date of laying in this case to about March the 28th or 29th. The hen bird differs little from the drake, but immediately I noticed that she had no white eye.

An odd diving duck then appeared and lived up to its name in true style, for it was under water as much as it was on the surface. I could not identify it, and as it was conspicuously marked about the head with a white stripe through the eye and a dark streak beneath it, I pulled out my notebook, and drew a rough sketch, from which T. later told me it was a female white-headed duck.

Finally, as though it were a secret to be revealed only when my patience had been proved, an astonishing noise from the depths of the reed bed took tangible form when a purple gallinule broke cover. Really, this is nearly as good a joke as a puffin. Only my surprise controlled a genuine laugh. In front of me twenty yards off stood a huge overgrown waterhen with brilliant red head and long red legs. It stood there, made its hideous noise and proceeded to rip up reeds which it ate forthwith. Bird, noise, gait, everything about it were just frankly funny.

APRIL 25TH. I spent the morning once again in my hide over the tree-nesting buff-backs, and exposed my usual complement of plates. I then had a sticky quarter of an hour in a changing bag, and with the new plates took a long series of general scenes. But no camera stands a chance of depicting this magnificence, and as I set about the task, I felt helpless. With a ciné something might be done. As it is, I have done my poor best. For the rest it must just remain a great memory.

I have not yet tackled the birds nesting in the reed bed. They offer much the best chance for photography, but I must have an old packing-case for a seat. As it is, this is T.'s last day, and I intend to get to work on them after his departure.

We assembled at lunch time and went over the scrub country on a general tour of inspection. En route, we saw a pair of woodlarks collecting nesting material and another roller—only the second we had seen. I now appreciate how fortunate we were to see so well that fine specimen on the fence post on my first evening in Spain.

This rough scrub-cum-ilex country constituted yet another of these small spurs which punctuate the edge of La Janda. In time it fell away again to the *vega* of the lagoon. In four old gnarled acacias were fourteen huge nests and eighteen storks to them. We decided on a closer inspection. This took us over an old stone bridge which spanned a small muddy stream, much to the consternation of a number of tortoises, which with remarkable agility plunged into the water.

Between us and the storks the only obstacle was now a field of bulls, but after the gentlemen of the Isla Menor these fellows were mere child's play, and soon we were at the nesting trees. The acacias looked the easiest things in the world to climb—until their thorns were experienced. They were the most vicious spikes I have ever encountered—huge things as sharp as needles. I tried one tree after another and got badly lacerated for my pains. When a thorn actually drove through a perfectly good leather sole and into my foot, I judged it time to give up striving to have a look at the inside of a stork's nest. I contented myself instead with sitting on the ground and watching the great birds swing back to their homes. They present a fine picture as they plane in on stiff wings, dropping their long legs afar off as if unsure what their balance will be.

We returned through the thicker scrub, and here I saw my first melodious warbler. This is a warbler of the *Phylloscopus* type, but it is larger. The views I got showed a yellow-breasted bird with brown upper parts, but it was impossible to see minute details of plumage.

APRIL 26TH–29TH. My last days have been spent with the reed-nesting buff-backs. The 26th was a *dies non* for birding, for we took T. into Seville to catch the night train north. That night P. and I also spent in a Seville which was so full that we had difficulty in getting a bed.

The next morning we returned to Vejer via Jerez where we managed to procure the much-needed packing case which acts as my seat in the lagoon, but only after much amusement. My Spanish is negligible; P.'s is quite good—but it does not run to the lengths required to explain either a packing case or the purpose for which we wanted it. The long-suffering grocer, the same from whom we had bought our stores for the *marismas*, was much perplexed—not unnaturally—by our demands, especially when I sat on a few in the shop to judge if they were of sufficient height to clear the water. Anyhow, we got one and left the good gentleman convinced that we were just another example of *locos Ingleses*.

On the afternoon of the 27th P. and I built a hide in the reed-bed colony over a nest which then contained two eggs. Since then I have been inside that hide nearly the whole time, emerging at intervals to plunge into a very hot and clammy changing bag to change my exposed plates.

Only two crises have arisen. The first loomed up as soon as we appeared—a 'local' from the near-by farm wading about the marsh with a basket on his arm into which he was dropping handfulls of buff-backs' eggs. Definitely not so good. He ignored our presence, and came solemnly past lifting every egg he saw, and in the end the two from my nest! . . . Expostulations followed. He could not understand it at all. Photographing birds? No, it was clearly useless trying to explain what I was up to. As he turned away, I nipped an egg out of his basket and popped it back in my nest. No wonder the biggest clutch I have seen up to date has been two. I take my hat off to any buff-back which gets as far as that without this human vulture seizing them. Doubtless there comes a day when he allows the birds to rear a brood—but

I certainly would not put it past a Spaniard ignorantly to kill the goose that lays the golden eggs. In any case, some of the nests in the sallows must rear broods, for they are on such slim branches that they could only be reached with difficulty, and with such abundance ready to hand I cannot see a Spaniard exerting himself to reach difficult sites.

The second crisis took more ominous form. Two obviously superior gentlemen came riding through the lagoon on horseback. I hesitate to think how many buff-backs' nests they destroyed. I imagine they were the farmer and a friend. At any rate they gave me to understand that I was trespassing. I heard something about *permicion*. I tried to explain by a sort of dumb show—camera, nest, bird flapping on to nest, click of shutter, photograph. Of course, it was just double Dutch to them. I think they realized what I was doing, but regarded it as positive proof of dangerous madness. These Spaniards strike me as being utterly blind to the things of nature. To them a bird is either edible or it is not. If the one, then one shoots it; if the other, one merely ignores it. However, I had no intention of packing up just when things were really beginning. To their further torrents of words my only answer was to shake my head to signify that I could not understand them—which was very true. At last they gave it up, and I got back in the hide. I was not again disturbed.

The buff-backs showed no fear as they tumbled back to their reed nests only to find them empty. Nor did they appear surprised that their egg or eggs had gone. I expect they are well trained to it by now, and take it for granted. Birds were all round me in a dense mass. My hide was semi-detached to an occupied nest, and before very long I felt rather than saw its owner creep back. My elbow was apparently in her nest. She gave it a shy tweak with her beak, and settled down on emptiness. After a while, I got my own back and gave her a quiet nudge as she sat, just to let her know I was still about. She prodded me with her beak again. We have been on such terms for two days—and all the time I have been changing plates inside the hide and getting out for a stretch every now and then. She flies away at this last performance, of course, but she does not seem to mind very much.

The birds on which my camera is focused are of course further

PLATE 20. KENTISH PLOVER (FEMALE) AT NEST

PLATE 21. KENTISH PLOVER APPROACHING NEST

PLATE 22. KENTISH PLOVER SITTING

off. They are both of them most obliging. The owners of a single egg, they are the proudest birds in this now barren community. They are so surprised about it that every now and then they both touch it together with their bills, then look at one another—absurd sight. Periodically one bird, the hen, I think (her bill is not so bright as her mate's) sits on the prize, as though to make assurance doubly sure that it is in reality there. Nor do I blame her. 'Sit while you can' would be a good motto for this heronry.

Both birds have been constantly present, and both have added bits here and there to their nest. Elsewhere in the reed bed is unceasing activity and a babel of noise. They are most quarrel-come creatures, and raids for building materials on a neighbour's nest are of common occurrence. No wonder each of these empty nests has at least one bird standing on guard. It would not last a minute without a sentry. As it is, they are so close together that when the sentinel turns its head away, the neighbour on the blind side makes full use of the opportunity and steals a bent! It is all most amusing, but at the same time a fearful shambles.

The climax came at my own nest. Both birds were standing proudly over their pale blue egg when a neighbour on the left could apparently stand such conceit no longer, for she leapt in at speed and in a trice had speared with her beak the solitary egg. Then and only then did I see the buff-back in full display. The dark plumes on the mantle were raised in a lovely delicate net-work above the back: the crown feathers stood up and out: the breast plumes were expanded. . . . And I hadn't got a plate left!

With that I packed up slowly and regretfully. It is difficult to tear oneself away from a scene such as this, but at last the wild olives and the coak oaks masked the heronry from sight as I struggled up to the road with my camera and hide. To-morrow it is Gibraltar and home. O that my job did not always tear me away from my bird haunts just as the nesting season is beginning in earnest!

A CAMARGUE DIARY

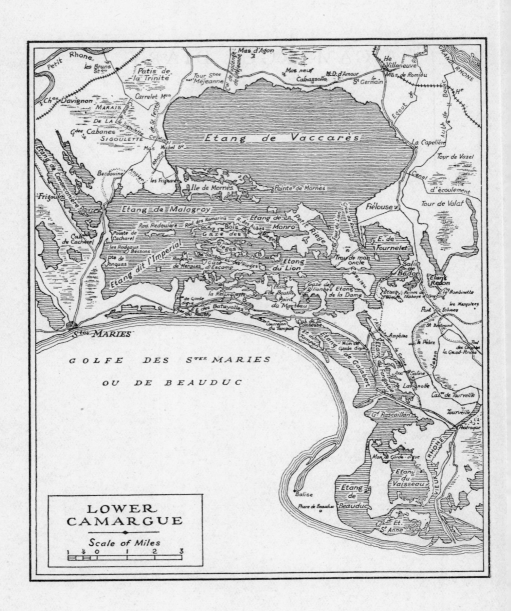

LOWER
CAMARGUE

Scale of Miles

1   ½ 0   1   2   3

A CAMARGUE DIARY

APRIL 23RD. To-day, my first in the Camargue, has been spent for the most part in getting my bearings. Geographically one is in the Camargue as soon as one crosses the pont de Trinquetaille over the Grand Rhône, for the region is clearly defined by the two arms of the Rhône which forks about a mile to the north of Arles—one river, the Petit Rhône, flowing down to the sea near Les Saintes Maries, while the other, the main stream, meets the Mediterranean at Port St. Louis. Of this large area we have to-day been exploring the eastern side.

For some eight miles due south below Arles the country, here called La Tête de la Camargue, is of no special note. The greater part of it has been subjected to thorough drainage and is now under cultivation, particularly of the vine. In its numerous dykes and occasional little swamps it is typical of all such reclaimed land. Tree and shrub growth is present but nowhere extensive.

Two surprises, however, were in store for us; the first, the funny little railway which connects with Arles Les Saintes Maries on the west and Salin de Giraud on the east; the second, the quality of the roads, even well down into the delta. Before I set out from England, from respect for P.'s car, I had made inquiries on this point, and the answers had not been encouraging—pot holes, mud up to the axle, and so forth. Yet to-day we have penetrated deep into the delta and found nothing in the way of road surfaces so bad as, for instance, one experiences on that so-called main road across the north of Scotland—a very agreeable surprise indeed.

In this cultivated area, in which we did not stop, I noted the ubiquitous corn bunting. Does one ever get away from this species? It was thriving here in great style. Skylarks also were numerous, and even as we sped by I had no difficulty in identifying by their characteristic rounded appearance several crested larks. Stonechats also were conspicuous, and magpies everywhere. For eight miles or so the car played with the railway a game of cross and re-cross, but at Villeneuve our ways parted, the track across 'the arids' to Giraud, the road down into the delta.

Villeneuve sees the end of the drained and cultivated area, and the beginning of what to me is the true Camargue, the saline *étangs*. Yet before we reached it, we stopped for a moment in a small wood and scrub 'copse' through which the road passes at the Mas de Romieu. Here we were nearly deafened by nightingales. They seemed to be singing from every bush, and indeed all to-day, wherever there has been suitable cover, nightingales have been singing, even well down into the delta. It is clearly, along with the magpie, one of the characteristic birds of the area. Goldfinches too were here very numerous.

Half a mile further down the road we at last reached the *étangs*, the Camargue which I had tried to imagine. A man's first sight of a promised land is always an occasion of note. To-day it came upon us very suddenly, for in this flat land a line of low tamarisks hides the horizon from view. As we rounded just such a clump, the whole scene changed, and we found the car running beside a huge inland lake—the Étang de Vaccarès.

My first impression was one of desolation, for waves of no mean order, lashed by the fury of the mistral, the accursed wind of Provence, were rolling up the muddy sides of the lagoon. Far across in the distance a thin line indicated the *étang's* far bank. North and south its coast line faded away into obscurity, and between us and the far shore white horses were breaking over the muddy water.

I must confess I have seen country which inspired me more—a feeling accentuated by the damnable blast of the gale. Even the sun, shining in true Mediterranean style, could not compensate for the miseries of being buffeted from side to side by the mistral. As we slowly crept down the eastern shore, which the road skirts, birds began to appear. We found them congregated, with some reason, in the sheltered bays, provided at convenient intervals by the small promontories of tamarisks and reeds which mark the spots where the main drains run into Vaccarès from the fresh marshes of the surrounding arids.

Here the first bird of note was a purple heron making heavy weather against the wind as, disturbed by the car, he rose from a ditch edge and made off into the marshes inland. Little egrets were especially numerous and conspicuous. They were fishing in both salt and fresh water, and we saw as many white heads and necks in the reeds of the marshes to the east as we did wading in the open *étang*. They were nervous and had no love for a car. Better even than in Spain, I now noticed their yellow feet. As the wading bird rises and draws its long black legs out of the water, the dangling yellow toes, when they in due course appear, are a misfit, a false and vulgar note in this beautiful bird's angelic plumage. But it is grand after two years to be back again in a land where the sight of a white heron cut against an ultramarine sky is a regular occurrence.

Rather to my surprise there were comparatively few waders, but Kentish plovers were much in evidence, twinkling over the muds on little black legs that moved so fast that the eye could scarce follow them. Their speed is truly astounding. Over the waters of the lagoon a Mediterranean herring gull planed on stiff wings, the yellow legs which characterize it clear to see against its white plumage. A solitary black-headed gull accompanied it. Several common terns were busy at their fishing, and I thought I saw a gull-bill farther out.

At the southern end of Vaccarès we stopped for a moment at La Capelière, the first of the three reserves set up in the Camargue by the French Société d'Acclimatation. We did not to-day introduce ourselves to the *garde*, but we noted for future examination the enticing reed bed which from here ran into Vaccarès. Thence past the promontory at Fiélouse until once again we met the lagoons—this time the Étang de Fournelet.

Here again we stopped, and I now turned my attention to the arids—*landes*, as they are called—which stretch away inland from the *étangs*. The ground is mud as hard-baked as a brick and cracked and scarred into weird patterns. It is plentifully grown with low bushes of *Salicornia*. Further inland dense reed beds hide away the often deep water of the fresh marshes with a prolific growth of feathery tamarisks.

Over the *marais* marsh harriers were quartering the ground in numbers equal almost to Spain. A hobby swooped over and sped

[71]

away on swift wings. But I was more interested in two small birds. Several fine cock ashy-headed wagtails occupied the highest perches, and I spent some time in satisfying myself that they were indeed of this sub-species and not migratory members of the typical *flava*, the true blue-headed wagtail. That they were probably ashy-headed their poorly marked eye stripes suggested, and I noticed too that the throat was very white with no visible traces of yellow.[1] Yet in the Camargue in April almost any of the many confusing sub-species of the yellow wagtail may be present on migration, and all call for close scrutiny.

In the same habitat (*Salicornia* scrub) I saw my first spectacled warbler. I was much interested in this bird, for from Glegg's list it is clear that it has been badly confused with the Dartford warbler. Superficially the confusion is understandable, particularly in its mannerisms. It has the same perky way of perching momentarily on a bush top and as suddenly vanishing into its depths. It carried its tail at the same impudent angle. Closer views revealed that it had a bluish grey crown to the head which shaded gradually into the browns of the back, and that its wings were a light reddish brown. Underneath the white of the throat gave place to a lovely pale pink breast—a most engaging little gentleman. The white 'spectacles' round the eyes, from which it gets its name, I think I imagined rather than saw. Certainly they do not constitute a good field character. Yet, when my scrutiny was over, I came away with the impression of a whitethroat rather than a Dartford warbler, and if the bird it to be confused at all, it should be with the former rather than the latter—but there are many species far more difficult to identify than the spectacled warbler.

Our next port of call was Salin de Badon, the centre of the Camargue sanctuary on the shores of Fournelet, and here P. and I introduced ourselves to Mon. Lomont, the *garde-chef*. He impressed me as a good ornithologist, certainly very systematic in his

[1] Mayaud (1938), from an examination of skins from the Camargue and the Eastern Pyrenees considers that the blue-headed wagtail breeding in the Rhône-delta is an intermediate form between the ashy-headed (*Motacilla flava cinereocapilla*) and the Spanish (*M. f. iberiae*). Field observations can never compete in such matters with museum work. I can only say that the Camargue wagtails are noticeably lacking in an extensive eye-stripe, which is one of the chief features of the Spanish form. As I do not know *cinereocapilla* in its typical locality (Italy), it is impossible to say more than that to my eyes at least the Spanish and Camargue birds are very different.

notes on the Reserve, for his answers to all our many questions were all carefully checked by him from his records of previous years. Apparently the year is a moderately dry one, though not exceptionally so. He had not yet, however, found any nests, but he gave us useful information to supplement that which I already had about the breeding grounds of the several species I am anxious to photograph.

Opposite Badon on the other side of the road was a small fresh lagoon from which, as we got out of the car, a purple heron had risen. From its antics and its squawks I had a strong conviction that it was breeding, for exactly like this did my Spanish birds behave with nests. So I donned thigh waders and started to search. My only reward, however, was a coot's nest with six eggs.

We then wandered along an ill-defined track beside a tamarisk-lined ditch. Almost immediately a Cetti's warbler bombarded us with its fiery song, but the bird itself remained the usual unseen songster. Truly this is an exasperating species to observe. We have to-day been constantly assailed by Cetti, yet never a glimpse have we seen of the warbler itself.

The track bordered on an area in which were two small fresh pools. On these were many waders—dusky redshank, wood and green sandpipers, greenshank, black-tailed godwit—but not a sign of a stilt, for which, at Lomont's advice, we had expressly come. I walked back over the *Salicornia*, where ashy-headed wagtails were frequent. I saw here also red-legged partridge and stone curlew. In a near-by reed bed were many mallard, and over it a kestrel was hovering.

From here we struck out along the southern shore of Fournelet towards the many small islets which the map marks in the middle of the *étang* region. Here in the tamarisks were many migrants, particularly spruce male pied flycatchers. A hoopoe slipped away like a huge tiger moth, and, alighting on the ground, immediately erected its crest. I saw too a cock redstart, a *phylloscopus* (willow wren, I think), a black-eared wheatear, and, most interesting of all, an ortolan bunting. Glegg's list does not even mention this species for the delta. Yet as a common bird in South France it is to be expected.[1] It was a fine cock with grey head,

---

[1] Since Glegg (1931) there have been many records, and Mayaud (1938) considers it a possible breeding species, and Glegg (1941) gives one record of a nest. The species breeds in the Alpilles.

yellow throat, and pinkish breast—very different from the drab ortolans I saw in Shetland in their non-breeding attire in autumn.

Our track eventually took us along a narrow strip of sand with open *étang* on either side. Here again were many waders—godwit, dusky redshank and greenshank, but above all avocets. There were many pairs, clearly not yet nesting, but by their constant chasings of one another obviously not far from it. What a joy they are to watch! Mallard, red-crested pochard, garganey (very numerous) and shoveler made up our duck list. A few great crested grebes rode the waters, and flying over Fournelet I saw many common, several gull-billed and one whiskered tern.

This preliminary inspection of Fournelet and the open delta was certainly encouraging. If time allows, we must don thigh waders and explore the islets far out. Some of them are well grown with low bushes, but most seem to be clothed only in *Salicornia*. For the moment we returned to Badon, and retraced our steps towards Arles.

Just north of La Capelière P. stopped the car to watch a pair of Kentish plovers which in a great state of excitement were chasing one another about on the edge of Vaccarès. In a few moments they both rose, flew across the road, and alighted on the hard-baked mud about twenty yards from the car. More chases followed, and then to my joy I saw the female run up to a scrape and shuffle down on to a nest. Inspection showed it to contain two eggs. The nest was a mere hollow in the dried mud and was utterly without camouflage except for an old dead *Salicornia* root. The scrape itself was lined with a few small shells, probably part of the cock's courtship offering. The two eggs bore no real resemblance to those of the ring plover, for they were without any gloss and buff rather than cream in their ground colour. We marked the nest for future reference. It had the merit of proximity to the road—but also the disadvantage of consequent publicity.

At Villeneuve we turned east on to the Giraud road, and started the old game with the railway. The country here is in part under cultivation, but is very dry indeed. Much indeed is just waste, although it is all drained. Magpies' nests littered the trees, even the low tamarisks, and one, with eggs, was only shoulder high and right on the main road!

When we met the Giraud road, we turned south again, our object the Ile des Pilotes, where the famous egretry is reported to be. We turned in at a sign post pointing the way to Auphan, and here I saw a fine male golden oriole. At the farm at Auphan I got into touch with the *garde*. Yes, indeed, the egrets bred here. To-morrow, early, he would be only too pleased to conduct us round the colony. It sounded promising. At that we called it a day, and not a bad first day either, for we have covered a good deal of ground and seen in all forty-four species—quite a useful start.

After dinner I called on Mon. Tallon of Arles, the local director of the Camargue sanctuary. He received me in a study in which was stored a mine of information. We talked for about an hour, or at least he did, for my French does not last much more than five, let alone sixty, minutes. But he was extremely helpful about many points, particularly the roads. In an area as vast as the Camargue it is well to know on first-hand authority what areas are practicable for motor transport. I gathered from him that his Society's detailed knowledge is more or less restricted to the three actual sanctuaries which it protects. As these are all on the eastern side of the delta, the whole of the Saintes-Maries side lies without their law, and they do not invade its privacy very much.

APRIL 24TH. Early away this morning, and the car was soon speeding down the excellent road to Le Sambuc. The mistral was again blowing its hardest. We stopped for neither birds nor scenery, and ere long we were again at Auphan. The *garde* was most hospitable. He is clearly used to ornithologists, a species of human being which, I imagine, has been a frequent visitor to him since this heronry was discovered in 1931.

I must confess that no fact of Camargue ornithology has impressed me more than this, that the exact breeding station of the delta egrets remained so long undiscovered. Glegg, for instance, did not know it, though he regards the bird as a nesting species. Yet the egret is a most conspicuous bird, breeds in big colonies, and furthermore is noisy at its breeding stations. Even so, the

Camargue egrets kept their secret from a competent ornithologist until as late as 1931. In all the reading about this area
which I have done before coming here nothing has impressed
me more than this fact. Even before I had arrived it had driven
me to the conclusion that the Camargue was a vast place. Now
that I have seen something of it I can understand the difficulties.

M. le garde had much to say about his birds—and of the
mosquitoes. Apparently not even the bird photographer was a
new form of freak to him, for only last year he had helped the
Dutch photographer, J. P. Strijbos, to work the egrets, and he
showed me some admirable photographs taken by him.

As we walked along the river wall—no Rhône could be seen—
I tried to take stock of this famous Ile des Pilotes. It could not be
called impressive. A long, dense line of trees marked the course
of the Rhône. Where the mighty river was I could only guess, for
neither sight nor sound of it was vouchsafed us all day. It is, of
course, obscured from view by the dense and extensive Congo-
like swamp of forest which fringes its banks. It was in this paradise for mosquitoes, according to the keeper, that the great
egretry was sited. I must admit that I was not a little perturbed by
the singular absence of birds. Not an egret was in sight. Yet in
here, said our guide, there were thousands. I pulled up my thigh
waders and plunged into the swamp, water up to my knees, and
mosquitoes, even in April, in numbers innumerable.

Yes, the keeper was right. There were thousands; nests festooned everywhere, some low pitched, some high . . . but there
were no birds. Is it always to be my luck to find my white
heronries deserted? First Spain . . . and now the Camargue.
Really, I think it time the gods of the chase gave me a break. I
emerged after a short, despondent search and reported to P. and
to the keeper. The latter assured me it was as yet too early.
Another week would see activity in full swing. I knew better.
This colony was dead, stone dead. No birds were going to breed
here in 1937. Otherwise some birds at least would have been
present.

The garde left us to our own devices at this point. P. and I
determined to inspect the remains. It felt rather like a cemetery.
Nests were everywhere, like grapes on a vine—but, alas, dead
things, mere shadows of the glory that a year before had graced

this dark, dank swamp. As we wandered through, we saw Strijbos' hide of last season. How convenient if the birds had been at home! But as we waded through the deep stagnant water, I knew that here we were faced with defeat. It is, of course, a matter of water level. From the accounts of friends who have visited this Pilotes colony one was lucky if the water did not come up to the waist under the breeding trees—in April, at least. Yet here were P. and I keeping dry in thigh waders. We wandered silently through the mortuary, and thence disconsolate back to the car. As we emerged two white crosses, egrets, were flying slowly over the trees. To me they symbolized flags at half mast.

We saw three wood pigeons here. Spring records for this species are apparently rare. It may be of some interest, but it is difficult to make the sight of a wood pigeon adequate compensation for the absence of egrets!

Our hopes crushed, we decided to revisit Salin de Baden. We continued down the Giraud road to Grand Badon and from there cut into Petit Badon. The map marked a road. We could only find dried mud, but it does not seem to matter much where one takes a car, so long as the chosen route is not blocked by scrub. The ground is so arid that there is no danger of getting stuck. After an amusing cross-country journey we finished up safely at Salin de Badon, though our good road of yesterday definitely stops here. South of Badon it is merely a mud track with great holes and rifts, but, with the ground so hard, quite serviceable for all that.

We spent some time pottering round Fournelet and Vaccarès. At Badon the first new species was a lapwing—not, I gather, a very common Camargue bird. In a tamarisk hedge I heard a quiet little *tsee-tsee* note which attracted my attention. The owner proved to be a penduline tit. It was as tame as I had been led to believe it would be, and it allowed me to examine it in detail at close range. The crown and nape are a soft grey, running into the rich red brown of the back. The light head contrasts strongly with the black patch across the eye. On the underparts it was light brown with fleckings of a richer shade—a most attractive little fellow with his absurd scorn for the human race not the least of his charms. He was much interested in the feathery

[77]

racimes of the tamarisks, but I could not see what exactly was inviting his attention. I hunted awhile for his remarkable nest, but without success.

On Fournelet were a few flamingo wading well out in the *étang*. How grand to see this wonderful bird again! Yet the flamingoes to-day were not so inspiring as those of the *marismas*. It seemed all wrong to be sitting in a car and watching their graceful actions. Nor did they fly, though an odd bird from time to time gave us a glimpse of its bright scarlets as it waved its wings.

Overnight the migrants have been coming in. I saw a few house martins; the pied flycatchers had noticeably increased in numbers. Many swifts were flying over, though yesterday there were none on view. But it was the woodchat shrikes which were most in evidence. Yesterday we had not seen a single specimen. To-day the tamarisks were overburdened with them. They must have arrived in huge numbers in the last twenty-four hours.

We pottered slowly back, stopping at frequent intervals to watch various birds. I spent more time with the glasses on spectacled warbler and ashy-headed wagtail. Near La Capelière we saw our first fantail warblers. We were attracted to them by their incessant little *chip-chip* alarm note which is uttered chiefly on the wing as the birds rise with weak fluttering flight. They are nondescript little warblers. In general the plumage pattern is reminiscent of a sedge warbler, but without the conspicuous eye stripe and with the light and dark browns of the back more contrasted.

Along the shores of Vaccarès and in the adjoining fresh marshes little egrets were very numerous. Yet their established breeding station was deserted. Surely it could only be that they had merely changed their quarters to some other part of the Rhône? I could not believe that they were all barren birds, for the water level, if apparently lower than usual, is nevertheless quite reasonably high. My experience in the Coto Doñana, of the buff-backs which formed a communal roost at evening near their breeding colony, came back to my mind. Did little egrets, by any chance, also have this habit of roosting at or near their nests? If so, would it not be possible to watch back to their roosts some of these many birds which by day were fishing out on the open delta? After dinner I would put the matter to the test.

At about 7.30 p.m. we took up our station first of all on the Giraud road at Le Sambuc. From here it was possible to see if the egrets were closing on the old colony. After all, it had been at a deserted breeding station that I had seen the Spanish white herons thus roosting. Gradually, however, returning flocks of tens and fifteens were noted. All were steering a course north of Pilotes; all, too, seemed to be flying in one set direction. It looked promising. I raced the car another mile up the road. Still more egrets were flying over towards the jungle by the Rhône. It looked better still. Another mile further on, by the big vineyard of Domain Giraud, the answer was in our possession. A steady stream of egrets were crossing over from the true Camargue. One and all were settling into the trees near a farm which the map marked as Tourtoulen. To make assurance doubly sure we ran the car down the mud road to the Rhône bank and walked along the river wall to the spot where the birds were congregating. Egrets were flying about in numbers, and amongst them I noticed the stumpy forms of several night herons. The dense tree growth prevented us from seeing if they were nesting, and obviously deep flood water made an inspection from under the trees temporarily out of the question. But I have little doubt that this indeed is a breeding station, and I am the more inclined to think so from the presence of the nocturnal night heron. After the shattering blow this morning at Pilotes this discovery has raised my spirits, and it is with impatience that I wait for to-morrow.

APRIL 25TH. We have spent all to-day in explaining and exploiting last night's discovery. We were away early, and were soon at Tourtoulen. I interviewed the farmer, and he had no objections, though clearly he could not understand what we wanted to do. He talked about deep flood water and high trees, but eventually left us to do our worst.

Clad in thigh waders, we set about a preliminary inspection. The first problem was the swamp. I tried to get through in many places, but the depth defeated me. At last, however, I found a way by which it was possible to get into the colony dry-shod, though only just. The water in one part laps the tops of our waders, but, thanks be, it can just be done. I should not like to have to strip. I do *not* imagine leeches are rarities in this part of the world.

This breeding station is very like the deserted one at Pilotes, and I confess that I see no valid reason why this should be occupied and the other abandoned. The water level here, if indeed slightly higher than at the old colony, is nevertheless very much the same—and the mosquitoes are just as numerous!

The nesting trees, chiefly alders and a few poplars, are growing out of the flood water. It is incredibly dense and dark, and as I plunged about to-day in the swamp I felt like a Stanley in darkest Africa, for it is a question of barging and pushing one's way through the network of old and rotten trees. Old boughs and branches liberally sprinkle the water and impede progress. Fortunately, once the first flood is negotiated, the main part of the colony is in reasonably shallow water, about knee high.

For some time we surveyed the colony. To estimate numbers is a profitless task. The tree growth is so dense that short of climbing individual trees it is impossible to compute the number of nests. Moreover, although the majority are occupied, there are also many old ones which have survived the winter. The area favoured by the birds, however, is comparatively compact—a patch of the swamp about two hundred long by a hundred broad. In this area nearly every tree has at least two or three nests so that without indulging in wild figures it can be realized that there are a considerable number of breeding birds. Again, it is difficult to estimate the proportion of night herons to egrets, but the latter certainly preponderate. The proportion is perhaps about four to one.

Nesting is well under way. Many egrets are obviously still building, but many, too, have started sitting, while the night herons are incubating hard, and have eggs, I imagine, well on the way to hatching. Without their owners I can see no real difference between either the nests or eggs of the two species. If anything, the night herons seem to build higher than the egrets, but this is not by any means invariable. Of many nests inspected to-day the majority held eggs. Most have four eggs, but there were a number with five.

After this exciting inspection I gave myself to the thankless

PLATE 23. NEAR LA CAPELIERE

The rank grass was the breeding ground of many pairs of Fantail Warblers and Stonechats
The undergrowth held Nightingales and Cetti's Warblers, and the fallen trees Penduline
Tits

PLATE 24. A CARMARGUE *LANDE* NEAR LES GRANDES CABANES

Black-winged Stilts, Pratincoles, Stone Curlews and Ashy-headed Wagtails were breeding
on this ground. Spectacled Warblers were characteristic birds of such *Salicornia* areas.
The tamarisks beyond mark the edge of the Etang de Consecanière. The hide is mounted
near a Stilt's nest

PLATE 25. HOOPOE (MALE) WITH CREST RAISED

task of selecting a site for photography. It might be thought that with so many nests to choose from this would require no thought at all. It has been, on the contrary, a most exhausting business. The trees are all as thin as laths, and with such slim branches that a secure perch for a tree hide is most difficult to locate. Often when an excellent nest and a suitable perch were located, it was found that three or four monarchs of the forest would need to be cut down to obtain a clear view. The great problem, indeed, is the density of tree growth. One is either too close, almost on top of the nest, or the view is thus obscured.

During the course of the morning I inspected at least eighty nests up about twenty trees. Each climb had to be done in thigh waders and with climbing irons mounted on top of them. By lunch I was played right out and thoroughly uncomfortable, sticky with sweat, devoured by mosquitoes, and swathed in the old spiders' webs which form a sort of barbed-wire entanglement between the trunks of the trees. But by lunch I had found my chosen site.

I lay stretched out for an hour on the river bank, and then carted all the tree hide materials, sacks, woodwork, etc., to the scene of operations. The site I have chosen has the advantage of controlling from the same hide one nest of night heron and several of little egret. The egrets in fact are something of an embarrassment, for there is one straight beneath the hide and one just up above. To right and left are several trees all with egrets in them, some no more than five feet away. From my chosen view point I am level with my night heron and have an excellent view on to an egret—though the angle down to it is rather acute.

This afternoon was, in short, a time of strenuous toil. I hesitate to think how many times I have scaled that poplar, but P. has been the real hero, for he has stayed below, attaching to my ropes my various requisites, and has thus drawn upon himself the full blast of the mosquito population.

Two hours' work, however, saw my tripod-stand set into position, all the wiring up finished, and the first sack pinned on to the framework. We gave the birds half an hour and then returned quietly to make sure that they had accepted the beginning of the hide. All was well. All the egrets, even those close to the sacking, and the single night heron were sitting happily.

F [81]

By now we had both had quite enough, and returned to Arles. In addition to our hide-building operations we found one nest of dabchick, with one egg, in the swamp water at the heronry. At the farm we saw two turtle doves, and also a pair of long-tailed tits. There are apparently very few records of this last species for the delta. I can only find two (April 1928 and April 1932). The birds were frequenting a tangle of scrub and are possibly nesting. Cetti's warblers and nightingales were both much in evidence along the Rhône bank, while I noticed a number of crested larks on the arids between Tourtoulen and the main road.

APRIL 26TH. The unspeakable mistral is still blowing! Does it ever stop? It is the more irritating when one looks up to the sky and sees the sun blazing out of cloudless blue. Everything in the garden would be rosy, were it not for 'the curse'. I would not mind if it was only content with making cold days which ought to be scorching à la Riviera. But it does not stop there. It blows a sandstorm into one's eyes; it rocks the car; it makes bird watching a misery, for it is frankly impossible to hold the glasses steady. Even the birds look all wrong, for they have to lean into the wind to keep their balance and thus become mere caricatures of their real shapes. Curse the mistral!

In such conditions it is a blessing to have our work centred at the egretry, for in the dark swamp it is at least sheltered. Even in the tree tops the growth is so thick that, although the sway is pronounced, it is enjoyable compared with walking out in the wind's full force.

Half the morning was spent at work on the hide. All the birds were sitting quite merrily on our arrival. I put another sack or so on to the framework, which now only needs a few extra patches, etc., for completion. After half an hour's absence we checked up. Both night heron and egrets were sitting happily. We then spent an hour in a further inspection of the colony. I climbed to a multitude of nests. I saw one clutch of six eggs—but whether egret or night heron I could not say—egret, I suspect, from its height.

We then made for Vaccarès to interview the *garde* at La Capelière—which we had been meaning to do for some time. Before we got there, however, we had a stroke of luck. Just by the railway halt at Villeneuve I saw a hoopoe beside the road with a grub in its long curved bill. P. stopped the car, and we watched. Scorning our presence in the Buick, it flew straight up to a perch on a wayside oak, not ten yards from us, and to my joy from out of the depths of a large hole I saw another long beak appear and take the food. The perch was about five feet up— ideal from my point of view, save that the road was unhealthily close for the curious.

Eventually we got to La Capelière, and met Mon. Bouisset, the *garde*. He is a delightful person, full of kindness and willing-ness to help, and although he has only a few acres of sanctuary under his control, what he does not know about it and its birds is not worth knowing. I do not know what he is like with the birds of the rest of the delta, but on his own ground he is superb.

La Capelière is a pleasant whitewashed house which is ap-proached down an avenue of tamarisks. Round it a few white poplars grow for protection. Behind it the reed beds of the inland *marais* grow; south is a tract of reed-grass-cum-*Salicornia*, a ter-rain where the marsh and the arid vegetation meet and vie with one another, mingling together in their rivalry. North is a small parched *lande*, and west beyond the road Vaccarès stretches away. In all it is but an insignificant little reserve, but it holds a host of small birds.

These we hunted up after Bouisset had insisted that we drank with him, met Madame B., and saw his dogs play their tricks. In the garden the swallows were busy in the outhouse: a goldfinch had a nest over the yard: Cetti swore at us from the dyke edge— and remained unseen. A nightingale was in full blast in the garden. In the *Salicornia* were a number of linnets—Mediter-ranean sub-species, of course—and we saw three nests with young. They were set nearly on the ground, deep in *Salicornia*. A stonechat—Continental brand again—had a nest from which the chicks had just flown. Right up against the road a spectacled warbler was sitting. As we parted the fleshy samphire, she peered up at us, but did not stir. In that quick view I saw clearly her 'spectacles'. Yet another nest by the road! If we go on like this, I shall get fat with lack of exercise when it comes to photo-graphy.

We saw two nests of fantail warblers. I have long wanted to see

[83]

this exquisite example of bird architecture. Nor was I disappointed. The nest is a marvel of subtle concealment and delicate construction. Not only is it composed mainly of spiders' webs, but these are woven round the living grass stems and thus form in the completed article a nest of the shape of an electric light bulb with the narrow entrance (about the size of a florin) where the bayonet grip would be. Its symmetry is perfect, and its camouflage beyond praise. Built, as it is, in the growing grasses, it is naturally part of them, and one needs to look twice to realize it is there at all.

One nest contained four eggs, but the interior was too dimly lit to see much of their markings. They looked bluish-white in ground colour with faint spots.

Another pair were building, and we watched the parents carrying in their material, long strands of web hanging from their beaks. They were exceedingly noisy while we were at their nests. The note is an incessant *chip-chip-chip*, highly irritating after a little time. It is uttered both on the wing and perched. The flight is weak, the bird mounting unsteadily from one perch and then quickly fluttering to another, as though deeming it unwise to trust its wings further. Despite good views I still find this a difficult bird to describe. It is so nondescript, patterned in light and dark browns on the wings, darker brown on the head, light beneath—a small sedge warbler without an eye stripe.

We now determined on a visit to the western shores of Vaccarès. So back to Villeneuve. En route we found our Kentish plover sitting hard, now on three eggs, and we watched a hen marsh harrier carrying building materials into an extensive marsh. When I went out to see if I could locate the nest, I found myself lost in a reed forest which towered above my head.

At Villeneuve we turned west along the north shore of Vaccarès. Here the road runs close by the *étang* and to the north the extensive Marais de la Grand Mar, which was a circling mass of marsh harriers. They were astonishingly numerous, but I cannot help remarking that in all the hundreds I have watched down here I have not yet seen one bird which for beauty and extent of its light markings can rival the solitary pair I saw at Hickling a fortnight ago! I wonder too why Montagu is a *rara avis* here— most curious. La Grand Mar offers much scope. Anything in-

PLATE 26. HOOPOE (MALE) WITH FOOD FOR SITTING FEMALE

PLATE 28. HOOPOE (MALE)

PLATE 27. STOAT AT HOOPOE'S NEST

deed could tuck itself away therein. As it was, we saw purple herons and egrets in some numbers.

At Méjeanne, which is a very arid area, we saw our first cuckoo on a tamarisk, and turned south for Carrelet and the Marais de la Sigoulette. I prefer this side of the Camargue. The country is arid to a degree, but it has a wilder atmosphere. Crested and skylarks were much in evidence, as also spectacled warblers, and near the dykes ashy-headed wagtails. The tamarisks were alive with migratory pied flycatchers and woodchats. Magpie's nests, old and new, were a feature of nearly every tree and bush! We watched a pair of stone curlews 'scrape-making' near Carrelet. The cock bird, after walking round the hen with half-raised wings, shimmied his breast into the mud. I did not envy him. It was as hard as a brick.

At the Canal Michel we stopped. This is a wide drain, carrying the water from the inland marshes into Vaccarès. Its banks were lined with feathery tamarisks, beloved of the penduline tit and tired migrants. We followed the track beside it. This was littered with dead carp which stank unto heaven. As the canal had a net across it, they were presumably rejected by the fisherman—but why he should just throw the poor creatures to rot in the sun instead of returning them to the water I cannot think. The stench was appalling. 'Smelly Alley' is now its appropriate name.

Two hundred yards up the canal I saw an extensive *lande*, hard-baked and with frequent but spaced tufts of *Salicornia*, and at the far end a pool. This proved to be the beginning of the Marais de la Sigoulette, and it is a regular bird paradise. Most noteworthy were the black-winged stilts. After failing to find them at the recognized breeding ground at Badon, I was beginning to fear that we should not meet with them at all, for they are not too abundant in the Camargue. Here they were, however, wading in the shallow pool. I watched again with joy that graceful high-stepping stride of the long thin red legs which is the very acme of grace and balance. I admired once more the smart distinction of their white bodies and black wings. Truly black and white in effective combination is a most attractive colour scheme for birds. Avocet, smew, great grey shrike—all of these owe much of their appeal to this simple combination of colours. In the stilt it is of course accentuated by the brilliant red legs.

These four birds were noisy, and I suspected breeding from the way they shrieked round us. I inspected the many little knolls of dry ground in the shallows but without success. It is, however, an ideal place, and I feel sure that they will soon be setting up house.

On this same pool were a number of black-tailed godwits and several common sandpipers. A sand martin was skimming the surface, while we flushed a common snipe from the bog. There are curiously few records of this species from the Camargue. I distinctly heard, but did not see, a whimbrel. A great spot this, and one which we shall certainly visit again.

APRIL 27TH. The mistral still! The only hope was the egret hide, though I doubted if even there conditions would be possible for photography. It is irritating beyond words, for we must soon be starting to break in our Kentish plover and hoopoe. But to think of mounting a ground hide in this gale is to court disaster. It would be blown straight out of the ground, however many guy ropes were used.

When we got to the egret hide, a big surprise was in store. All the egrets were sitting contentedly and happily, but from the nest which, when we left yesterday, had been occupied by a night heron a little egret rose! Surely it cannot be that it is a case of inter-breeding? A nice thought—night heron and little egret in hybrid form!

I occupied the hide for a few hours with my camera to see if I could make anything of this strange ménage, and also to watch the reactions of my egrets to the hide and my lens. P. had hardly moved off when the egrets tumbled back with much swearing and squawking to their nests. They have all the uncertainty of our own grey heron in the tree tops. They alight gingerly, as if unsure of their balance. They peer down at the next perch on the way to the nest. They fix it with their sinister yellow eye. The head and neck jerk up and down in uncertainty. At last they take the plunge, and so on until the nest is reached.

Within five minutes all my egrets were sitting and quite unperturbed, even the good lady immediately below my hide, who by cocking her head sideways could look straight up at me from the bottom. She did so often, but did not seem to recognize in my nether portions anything human. I felt slightly insulted!

For twenty minutes there was no sign of my night heron. Then to my amazement on stalked the egret and settled down to incubate. What is one to say? Yesterday when I left this hide, a night heron was sitting those eggs, now an egret! Well, there it is! Perhaps I shall get more evidence later. For the moment I rested content with what the gods of the chase had presented, and got busy with my camera.

It was a great moment to have this bird at last a few feet from me, and my mind went back to those days at Vejer, when I had seen my first egrets nesting amongst the buff-backs and had then sworn that one day I should sit close to this bird. Those who cast scorn on bird photography and who regard it as a waste of time can know nothing of the thrill of successfully outwitting a species which has long been desired and for which one has had to work hard and travel far. The simple bird watcher is content with his views through glasses. The egg collector takes the chase one further and tracks his quarry to the nest. The bird photographer has to advance one further step, and smuggle himself to within a few feet of his subject. Every bird I work brings me a great thrill as first I see it approaching, but when it is one, like this egret to-day, which has been a long-standing ambition, then great indeed is the reward.

When P. came up to relieve me, the usurper was still sitting. There had been very little activity in the intervening two hours. All the egrets had just sat, occasionally turning the eggs, but at one nest, unfortunately rather hidden by foliage, I had the luck to see nest-relief take place. This was a noisy performance, but it produced a magnificent display of plume-raising. These lovely 'ospreys' are so fine and delicate that as they lie, white on white, along the back they are hardly discernible. When the mate arrived, both birds erected them until they looked like two brides hanging with trains of gorgeous lace. Only the vulgarity of their squawks spoilt the aesthetic effect, and indeed even this cacaphony of ill-sound could not really destroy the loveliness of the ceremony. Apparently, then, both sexes help to incubate—although I cannot separate cock and hen.

[87]

To-day in the egret swamp I heard several wood wrens. At least, they half-sang the wood wren trill. They started off as though working up for that lovely crescendo that on a hot June day is like a freshening waterfall to tired ears. But with these wood wrens the water only bubbled up; it never fell. As there was a number of them, it is most odd that not one got further than the introductory notes. I cannot help feeling that there is something wrong about them. Are they Bonelli's warblers? In the glasses they look just like wood wrens, but then plumage distinctions are never the best means of identifying the *Phylloscopus* family. I fear they must remain, for the present, of doubtful species—wood wrens, with a question mark against them.

When we emerged from the dank and dark, we found the mistral lashing the open with full fury. For the rest of the day we pottered rather half-heartedly. Watching birds in this gale is no fun. One's temper is less frayed sitting in Arles. However, we watched our hoopoe for a little while to see how frequently he fed. We waited an hour. He came with food at three-forty, three-fifty, four-thirty—quite a good husband to his sitting wife.

For the rest we watched a few birds in their misery on exposed Vaccarès, but got little amusement from it. Even the car rocked in the wind. Our only new species to-day has been green woodpecker.

To-night Scop's owls have been very noisy in Arles, especially in the main street. As we sat in our café after dinner, they were calling to one another on all sides—an unmistakable *klu-klu*, quite easy to imitate, and the birds play up well, responding to even the most amateur efforts of human mimicry.

APRIL 29TH. Yesterday, the 28th, the mistral excelled itself. We decided to give the Camargue a rest. We donned our better garments and became good tourists—a pleasant enough day, but not a birding one, and therefore without a place in my diary. To-day, the gods be praised, the mistral is dead. And there have been no tears at the funeral. The Camargue has been at its best, and for the first time, since it has blown incessantly from our arrival, I have appreciated the truth of the adjective iridescent which an American writer has applied to this odd corner of France. To-day we have seen a Vaccarès that was picture-post-

PLATE 29. PENDULINE TIT CONSTRUCTING NEST

PLATE 30. PENDULINE TIT BUILDING INTERIOR OF NEST

PLATE 31. PENDULINE TIT BUILDING OUTER WALL OF NEST

PLATE 32. LITTLE EGRET

card blue, a Vaccarès still and unruffled by even the faintest breeze. Mirage has appeared and cheated sight and sense by drawing railway trains on the horizon. The feathery tamarisks no longer have their delicate tresses blown furiously in the gale; they hang peacefully, pink at their tips. The birds too are now more scattered. They no longer walk and fly as though leaning on the wind. They have left the sheltered bays and are out on the open flats. To-day the Camargue has truly smiled. It has been hot, of course . . . but that was to be expected. I prefer a roasting to the return of the mistral.

We have put this, our first calm day, to good account. I opened with six hours' work on the egret, with both my still camera and P.'s ciné. Something has happened to the night heron. Quite what I am at a loss to say, for she was certainly all right when the hide was completed. Now she is just not there, nor was the usurping egret. I can only now suppose that it was not a case of *mésalliance* (not that I ever seriously imagined it to be so). Probably the usurper was a cock egret without a job on hand, or perhaps a hen bird which had lost its clutch or was barren. The mystery is the stranger because all the egrets round the hide, even those which are almost semi-detached, are as happy as could be.

On one of these I have been working most of to-day. Even six hours has produced very little incident, however. The birds were back as soon as on the last occasion—within five minutes of P.'s departure. They returned and sat, and that is about all there has been to it. Those who imagine a bird photographer has unrivalled opportunities for observing habits and behaviour ought to sit for six hours on a few species. They would be surprised how inactive they can be!

While I was working with my own camera I got no opportunity to get pictures of the egret with its plumes raised—to my great disappointment. When I took over with P.'s ciné the bird was most obliging, and spent its time in half-raising its 'ospreys'. At close quarters the little egret is a lovely thing, but in its make-up it has two false notes. The long slender serpentine neck surmounted by that yellow eye and rapier-like black bill gives it a most sinister expression which ill accords with the angelic innocence of its virgin purity. Not content with this contradiction,

[89]

nature has been unkind in garbing the gouty toes at the end of its black legs in a pair of bilious yellow socks—a most unfortunate detail aesthetically.

The flood water at the egretry is definitely decreasing—but not the mosquitoes! If it declines at this speed, I am wondering what will happen to the dabchicks. We found another with eggs to-day. They will certainly be short of water before they hatch, even though at the moment it is knee deep at least at their floating nests. My strange wood wrens are still present in numbers and still singing their curious half songs.

We spent the rest of the day in making up for lost time in starting our hides on the hoopoe and Kentish plover. On both these hides, in view of their proximity to the road, I stuck up large notices in my worst French, *Ne touchez-pas, s'il vous plaît*. But with the curious the main point is to satisfy the inquisitive instinct. So I added, *Cabane pour photographier les oiseaux*, which I thought a pretty tricky piece of French for me, especially the word for a hide, which had me properly foxed! To give weight to these explanations I signed myself *Société Zoologique de Londres et Société d'Acclimatation de France*. As P. said, it sounded important, and those who read it were not to know that it was untrue in both particulars! Yet without some explanation I felt the hides, particularly the hoopoe one, would not stand a day. It would not be the first time a bird photographer's tent has been commandeered in the Camargue!

Most of the rest of the day was spent in checking up on these two birds to see that they had accepted the strange erections. Both hides were, of course, set up at a distance of about eighteen feet. The Kentish plover apparently regarded such things as all in the day's work, for she was soon incubating, and we were able to make another move before evening and set it up at twelve feet. The bird returned as soon as we were in the car!

The hoopoe was very much more shy. After all, it was only the cock feeding the hen, and I dare say he felt that she could come out and find her own food. I felt a certain male understanding for that bird. At last, however, he flicked on, fed her quickly and was away. We left him to get over his fears.

We have seen only two new species to-day. Near La Capelière a few bitterns were booming. It is rather strange that there are

not more. Doubtless they have been until to-day suppressed—
and depressed—like ourselves, by the mistral. Anyway, they
were in good voice this afternoon. The second species was a kingfisher—not very remarkable, perhaps, except that there do not
seem to be many records for the delta. But the way in which it
introduced itself made its sight the high spot of the day. It came
flashing out of a marsh drain, swung over Vaccarès, and there
hovered like a tern, flashing the colours of a rainbow in the brilliant light. It was a fitting gesture to the sunny loveliness of this
perfect day.

APRIL 30TH. Up early and in the hoopoe hide. The light is only
on the perch by the nesting hole from 8 to 9.30 a.m., so that
sessions are naturally short. The cock bird is shy. He definitely
does not like the evil eye of my lens. However, he is feeding his
lady at reasonable intervals, but he does so with astonishing
speed. He flicks on to the perch and is off before one can say
knife, but not before he has handed over the food to his ever-
hungry mate. Her appetite indeed is most hearty. She seems to
have an unending stomach to fill. When her lord was absent for
some forty minutes this morning, she started swearing audibly in
the depths of her hole—a strange noise, rather like the chattering
of young woodpeckers but less hurried in its delivery. When this
spasm of indignation failed to produce him, she herself emerged,
was absent for five minutes and returned without so much as a
glance at the hide. She at least has no fears about the tent. I wish
her husband had her courage.

My visions of him this morning have been confined to mere
flashes. As he flicks on to the perch, his black and white wings
seem huge—but he is a lovely thing, all decked out in pinks—a
big tiger moth. When getting up courage to visit the perch, he
spends much of his time standing in the road, and it is here I
have had my best views of him. His crest is usually carried flat on
his head, but is often erected just as he settles. It is pink brown
like the rest of him, but each feather of the fan has a black dot at
the tip.

For the next four hours both P. and I were busy on the
Kentish plover. Curiously enough she did not greatly mind the
drone of the motor of P.'s ciné, but she disliked the steady gaze of

my lens. This was not a little disappointing, for she has so far behaved to the unoccupied hide in exemplary fashion. No doubt she will prove to be like all the ring plovers I have worked—most obliging when one is not in the hide, equally infuriating when one is within. To-day she has obliged, but rather unwillingly, and I have not pushed her hard. She was sitting quite happily when we left—as soon as the lens was removed, in fact. Both birds were close by the nest, but the cock's task was that of my ally, trying to chivvy his unwilling lady on to her eggs. There is more difference than I thought between the sexes. He has more black on him, particularly on the head. His collar too is bolder and more clearly defined.

Thence down to La Capelière where we spent the rest of the day. In our wanderings we saw much, but nothing that has been new. I spent most of the time enjoying the sun, watching fantails, spectacled warblers and ashy-headed wagtails. I also got obstinate about Cetti and determined to see this elusive warbler, but except for glimpses I got no further than in the past, both in Spain and here! Is there any bird more elusive and more skulking? It would be less irritating if it had not that powerful song which seems to throw out a perpetual challenge—'What-yer—what-yer — what-yer — Come-and-see-me-bet-you-don't — bet-you-don't!' or so its mocking sounds to my ears.

One success, however, we did have. Just off the reserve ground at La Capelière up a dyke heavily grown with tamarisks Bouisset showed us the nest of a penduline tit—or *remiz*, as the French so much more attractively call it. He had found it only that morning, and it was building. It was the bird's second attempt, for the first nest, nearly completed, lay on the ground beneath the tree, a victim of the mistral's fury. I imagine that many of their efforts must thus come to grief.

The nest is another marvel of bird architecture. It is built into the pendent and feathery down-hanging sprays of tamarisk, and is a domed ball of reed fluff. The destroyed nest was nearing completion, and was much like a long-tailed tit's with reed 'down' for lichen and moss in its materials. The new nest had not advanced far in its construction. An outer circle, as it were, is first built into the tamarisks. This is the foundation upon which the birds built up the main walls. These are apparently con-

PLATE 33. LITTLE EGRET

PLATE 34. LITTLE EGRET IN THE TREE TOPS

structed upwards from the bottom, and evenly on both sides. This was the stage at which the birds had to-day arrived. As we watched them, they were framed in a window, for most of the building was done from inside the growing nest, and as the back has not yet been filled in, they were silhouetted clearly against the sky behind.

The penduline tit is a *most* attractive bird. Ridiculously tame, it allowed us to stand ten feet off—the nest is about seven feet high—and watch it at its work. Both sexes take part in this task, and they toil without a break, arriving at frequent intervals with their beaks full of fluff. As though distrusting their joint weights on the tamarisk spray, they never appeared together on the nest, one always waiting until the other had completed its work and flown away for more materials. All the time they call to one another—a quiet little *tsee-tsee-tsee*. It had a ring of subdued excitement beneath it.

We have now seen or heard *remiz* in many places, but it is to be noted that always they have been over water, if only a dyke. They are wholly absent from the tamarisks which grow in the arids. This is their favourite tree, but they are not exclusive to it. We have seen them in the poplars round Bouisset's house and again in the dense jungle of the egretry, although we have not found a nest there. It would indeed be no simple task in this last locality.

The nest was ideal for photography—apart from its constant sway as the birds were working. It required a ladder, and this the good Bouisset immediately provided—a strange home-made affair, but serving its purpose admirably. We set it into place, but built no hide. I do not think *remiz* will require one. If necessary, a sack over my head should do the trick when the time comes—but it will need to be a very windless day.

MAY 1ST. Our programme has been much the same as yesterday. From 8 a.m. to 3 p.m. both P. and I have been working on the hoopoe and the Kentish plover. The former has gained a little confidence but is still shy. I imagine the cock bird will always be timid, for he has very little real pull to make him come to the nest. However, we satisfied ourselves that the hen is getting her fair share of food! The trouble is not so much that the cock will not come to feed her, but that his stays on the perch are only momentary. Indeed it is astonishing how quickly he manages to hand over the food.

The Kentish is behaving just like the worst type of ring plover —perfectly tame when the hide is unoccupied, but nervous about the lens. However, while I was in the hide—and it is incredibly hot inside!—P. watched another bird back to a nest higher up the road. We have duly tented this in the hope that she may prove a more tractable subject than our present one.

This new nest is in similar country, but is far less exposed. Low tufts of *Salicornia* cover the ground, and the scrape is at the foot of one of these. The three eggs are half-buried in the ground and are an excellent example of protective coloration. So far to-day she has reacted in exemplary fashion to the proximity of the hide —but so did Kentish No. 1, so that I am counting no chickens until I have seen how she behaves in front of the lens.

En route from Villeneuve to La Capelière in a bay at the north end of Vaccarès we caught sight of about a score of flamingoes feeding. As they were protected by a line of tamarisks I spent some time in stalking them with the big lens. One small lot I worked up to in the best deer-stalking style and through the tamarisks got a few exposures. The main body were less screened and the best I could do was to crawl forward, walking the three legs of the tripod in front of me! The birds were wary and, although they refused to fly, they have the best possbile idea of what constitutes a safe distance, and this they are careful to keep by the simple process of wading further out into the *étang*.

We watched them feeding—memories of the *marismas*! Once again I admired the elegance of the slow movements of their long pink legs. They have perfect balance as they bend their 'knees' and stride forward. So gently is the leg returned to the water that it seems the bird is anxious not to create a ripple. When feeding, it presents an extraordinary doubled-up appearance, for the thin sinuous neck is plunged into the water at the bird's feet, and gives it the impression of a round body on three legs! From the wriggling of the neck I imagine the heavy bill churns up the mud to stir up the crustaceans which are the flamingo's food.

At La Capelière we inspected the penduline tit—and ran into

unexpected trouble. As we emerged on to the road, an old bone-shaker drew up, out of which a be-bracered, shirt-sleeved Frenchman emerged. He was clearly very angry, and poured voluble French into my uncomprehending ears. After about five minutes' flow I managed to get a word in edgeways and to convey to him that my French did not reach such a standard. Whereupon he started all over again! Very distressing. This time I managed to hear a few words about *cabanes* and *oiseaux* and gathered our activities were the cause of the trouble. So I persuaded him to visit Bouisset at La Capelière.

B. played up like a man, but he was at a physical disadvantage, for the irate gentleman towered over him, and with thumbs stuck in his braces and his fingers twitching all the time he swore, cursed and rated the unoffending Bouisset. I did not actually time him, but I am prepared to swear he did not stop for a quarter of an hour. When finally he ran out of words, he leapt into his car before B. could reply. This he backed at such speed that the chickens had to move like lightning to avoid total destruction.

It was ridiculously funny, and so was the sequel. P., who speaks no word of French, seized the steering wheel, made gestures of drinking, and out came the irate gentleman as benign as a lamb! Half an hour later, after thirsts had been quenched, there were handshakes all round, and we were authorized to go where we pleased! I gathered from B., when we had recovered, that the objection was our Kentish plover hide. As it was within ten yards of the road on a stretch of bare mud, it seemed little to get so hot under the collar about! But marvellous indeed are the powers of alcohol!

Neither the spectacled nor the fantail warbler had hatched, so we did not yet build hides on them, which had been our intention. Several cock spectacled warblers, however, were feeling in good fettle at the return of the tranquil weather. They were hurling themselves up from the top of the bushes singing lustily, very like whitethroats in all respects. By a grass-grown dyke-side we saw yet another nest of fantail. It contained five eggs.

We spent the rest of the day out beyond Salin de Badon and the southern end of Fournelet towards le Cassieu. We were particularly concerned to see if the avocets had yet set up house. They were in the same spot—an area of rapidly drying mud, and were exceedingly noisy and demonstrative, but extensive watching gave no proof that a pair yet had eggs.

This area beyond Badon is most fascinating. Birds were exceptionally numerous, and although we only added one new species (common whitethroat) to our list, we were never without something to look at. Ducks, particularly mallard, were in numbers, and a few red-crested pochard, fine drakes with their light heads and black breasts. Off a point of land I counted eighty-odd flamingo feeding and further over sixty or seventy more. Gull-billed terns seemed more common than on our last visit. The tamarisks were full of migrants. Really the pied flycatcher passage here has to be seen to be believed. Woodchats, too, are common, but the movement, so noticeable the other day, is now less pronounced and clearly many have already moved through to the north.

MAY 2ND. We started with the usual hoopoe session. In view of the brief period for which the light is actually on the perch this looks like being a regular task every morning. The cock hoopoe is more used to things now, and this morning he has been feeding at regular intervals, but he never stays for more than a flash. As if to celebrate the recovery of his nerves, he serenaded me from the next tree with his monotonous *hoop-hoop*.

I had a visit from the local children of Villeneuve. They stood and stared at the hide until from within I shouted '*Allez vite.*' They *allez*-ed all right, believe me. I do not think that hide will be disturbed again!

While I was in the hide, P. spent the time in watching a pair of fantails carrying building materials. He found the nest, and I examined it later. It was much the most perfect example of this bird's architecture we have yet seen. Being in the ditch side, it was less well concealed than the nests in the long marsh grass. Its delicate symmetry was marvellous. The habitat, too, was not without interest, for up to now we have found this species only where the big *marais* begin to merge into the arids, i.e. in marshy fields. This new nest, however, was in a very dry area, although the small ditch provided a little of the marsh atmosphere.

Thence to *remiz*. The camera had first to be lashed on to the ladder, and when this was done, I threw a sack over my head, and soon made a number of exposures on the confiding pendulines. For all their tameness they are a photographer's nightmare. They move like lightning and are never really still. Moreover, their movements, if not the breeze, make the pendent nest sway badly. However, I have made many exposures and hope that some of the negatives at least will not show the annoying blur of movement.

Both birds were again active in building. Most of the work is done from inside the growing nest. The material is pushed into place with the bill, and very vigorous are the thrusts with which this is carried out. From time to time the bird climbs about the outside to see that everything is ship-shape.

I have little to add to the notes I took the other day on plumage. The head is a light grey, almost dirty white. The shoulders and back are rich brown, the underparts light brown and flecked in a darker shade. He has too a bold black patch on the head which contrasts strongly with his light crown. In the reed bed close by we heard a pair of bearded tits. I am rather surprised that this species is not more abundant.

We were now clear to inspect more of the western and southern sides of the Camargue. For up to date we have only covered a part of the east of the delta. We turned north, and at Albaron got on to the road to Les Saintes Maries, where at last we sighted the Mediterranean, not looking its established ethereal blue—despite a lovely sky above. From Les Saintes Maries the maps mark a most questionable road which threads its way across the *étangs* and islands, and between them and the sea. According to Tallon this was passable, despite appearances. It was obviously a most convenient road for bird watching, if it could be used, for it skirts the southern edge of the remote Étang dit l'Impérial and the Étang du Lion.

We risked it. It started as a track in the sand and then improved slightly, but it was never more than just over a car's width across and at several of the bridges (sluice gates) we could only just get the Buick through. At its eastern end it runs as the only bit of dry land between the Étangs of Fangassier and Galabert. Here the road looks like a long low pier, for on either side it is protected against the waters by a line of thick massive stakes. In short, it is really a remarkable piece of engineering, though

G

quite whatever persuaded the authorities to construct it remains a mystery. But 'Theirs not to reason why'; for bird-watching it is a godsend.

Along this southern road, on the stake posts and in the few tamarisks, migrants were at their best, as one would expect so close to the Mediterranean. Except for the sand dunes between the road and the sea it is their first stopping place. Here were, of course, the inevitable pied flycatchers and woodchats. Several wheatears used the road stakes. Redstarts too were often thus perched, while whinchats were especially numerous.

The two most interesting species were a cock black redstart and a male rock thrush. I first spotted this last in the middle of the road. It is the first I have seen, and I must confess its colour scheme is a little overwhelming! Head and throat are a rich light blue, and the underparts orange. The wings are dark, and contrast sharply with the white patch in the middle of the back. The whole bird presents a strange appearance, rather garish to my taste. For all its brilliance I cannot say that it is a bird with a strong aesthetic appeal. It is too patchy and too elaborate.

On the *étangs* were many flamingoes, and avocets in abundance, though they showed no signs of nesting. On an island in the area called La Relanguette were countless common terns and a number of gull-bills. I waded across, but so far they have not yet laid. The flamingoes here let me approach very close indeed. Mediterranean herring gulls and a few black-headed were also recorded. On the dunes we saw a single oyster-catcher, which, I gather, is not a common species in the Camargue and is confined to this area.

At the eastern end of Fangassier the road petered out and we had to find our way back to Badon as best we could over the dried mud. Here at le Pèbre we saw our first examples of the famous Camargue bulls about which I had been frequently warned before leaving England. After Spain I merely scorned them—from inside the car, of course!

To-day's circular tour has at last enabled me to form a complete mental picture of the delta. Enclosed within the two arms of the Rhône are in the main three types of country. The top end of the triangle of the delta (la Tête de la Camargue) is arid, drained marsh, considerably cultivated both for vines and for cereals. Here tree and shrub growth are quite a feature of the landscape, although nowhere can anything like a wood be descried. The central area is devoted to the *étangs*. These are in reality all one, but broken up into differently named lagoons by a sea of small islets which become more numerous as the Mediterranean is approached. Here *Salicornia* is the dominant vegetation. On either side of the *étangs* there stretches away to the two Rhônes an arid area (*landes*) plentifully sprinkled with heavily reed-grown marshes, of varying size and depth of water. This ground is liberally grown with tamarisks. As the rivers are approached, the land is brought more under cultivation and trees again become more in evidence. Along both rivers run thick lines of trees almost jungle-like in their density. The southern littoral is an area of low sand dunes intersected by several saline *étangs*—a veritable wilderness.

MAY 3RD. A day of almost solid photography. I opened up as usual on the hoopoe, which is now far more tractable. We then spent the rest of the morning working on the new Kentish plover. She is certainly a better bird than our old friend, but even so does not like the lens. Without it she is quite happy and returns immediately in front of the hide. Watching through my peep-hole, I saw another Kentish running through the *Salicornia*. At first I thought it was the mate to my bird, but I then saw it was another female. She stepped on to a nest not fifteen yards away from my own. Subsequent inspection showed it to contain the usual clutch of three.

P. then went into the *remiz* hide. As we plunged through the reed bed on the way to it, I got a fair view of my first little bittern. The bird on the wing shows much black and a deal of white, but exactly how the two were intermingled I did not have time to see before it plunged into the cover of the reeds.

The fantail has hatched, and we put a hide up on her. Now that there are chicks, the parents incessantly give tongue with their alarm note. I shall be much interested to see how the bird gets in and out of that small entrance hole.

The rest of the day I spent aloft with my egrets. They are certainly dull in behaviour during the incubation period. Despite a long session to-day I have seen nothing of any note—not even nest-relief, which I hoped I might get again at my nest. In short, it has been a busy day, but with so much time spent in hides that there has been little for field work. The only new species have been little bittern and a little owl near Tourtoulen.

MAY 4TH. Needless to say I started with my usual hour and a half on the hoopoe. The cock is now quite reconciled to the operations of photography. But he was not the only visitor to the nest perch to-day. In the middle of the session I was astonished, and not a little alarmed, to see a stoat appear! Where he came from goodness knows. He must have climbed up the blind side of the tree. The first I saw of him was occupying the exact spot where the cock alights. In case I was dreaming I made an exposure which I trust in time will prove that I was not suffering from hallucination. He then turned round and vanished—for all I could see into the nest hole.

I was naturally much concerned about the safety of the sitting female. It seemed impossible that the little villain had not scented her. Yet ten minutes later the cock appeared, and to my relief I saw his lady's long beak come out of the hole and take the food. The incident sets a pretty problem. Can it be that sitting birds have no scent? Or is it true, as I have heard, that hoopoes give off such an offensive scent that no beast will go near them? All very mysterious.

The rest of the morning was spent upon the fantail. As P. said, it is not a very remarkable bird to look at. I must agree. Even now, after several hours within a few feet of it, I am still left with my earlier feeling, that it is a nondescript, cleaner-coloured sedge warbler—smaller, of course. At close quarters I saw that the head is dark, the brown feathers almost obscuring the buff ground colour, that the heaviest brown markings occur on the wings, and that the rump is tawny.

Yet I was interested in its behaviour. In the grass it acts just like a bearded tit, slithering up and down the reed stems, and it is an even greater lover of 'the splits'. Indeed it is exceptional for it not to perch with one foot on one grass stem and one on another. After each feed it carefully worked its way up the grasses and from the top surveyed the landscape o'er, to see that all was clear before flying off. Feeding was non-stop, at intervals

PLATE 35. LITTLE EGRET

PLATE 36. BLACK-WINGED STILT (FEMALE)

PLATE 37. BLACK-WINGED STILT (FEMALE)

of about five minutes, and both sexes took part—not that I can separate male and female in the field, but I saw both at once carrying food. After every few feeds the nest is cleared of excreta, which is carried off in the bill. The birds go right into the nest to feed, turn round inside and come out head first.

From La Capelière we headed for the stilt ground near the Canal Michel. But before we got there much had happened. We opened with a great tit at Villeneuve—not a very exciting start. On Vaccarès we saw a grey heron (Tallon, when I saw him to-night, was very excited about this! Apparently it is very late for them).

Close by the road a little further on, where the reeds of the extensive Marais de la Grand Mar abutted on to a long fresh pool grown with tamarisks, were a herd of horses. Amongst them I saw a white heron running. Surely not a buff-back in the Camargue? There are no records at all that I can find.[1] I must confess that when I saw its buff plumes I thought it must be a squacco. But no squacco ever chased livestock in that fashion. Only buff-backs played that dancing game. Buff-back he was—records or no records. P. shot some film of him as he ran after his equine friends.

More surprises were in store for us when we turned south again at Méjeanne. In the first bay of Vaccarès was another grey heron. The same bird? He might, I suppose, have flown across the *étang*. But it was not the heron we stopped to look at, but a fine osprey busy at his fishing. What a superb creature! Dark brown of back, white of stomach, and light on the head, he looked grand as he sailed over the water. But it was as nothing to the grandeur of his plunge. This he does with wings folded above his back, and with his big talons stuck out at full stretch. The angle of his dive was gradual. There was nothing of the gannet's nose-dive. He glided into the water at about sixty degrees, albeit at a goodly speed, and great was the splash of his impact. He failed to catch. Of the osprey, too, there seem to be few records. To-day the gods of the chase have been kind.

They were to be kinder still before we were done. Before we

[1] Mayaud's paper (1938) gives two records for this species for the last century, and the *Actes* (1932) mention a possible occurrence in October 1931.

reached 'Smelly Alley' we had seen yet two more new species (to us) for the delta. Three lesser black backed gulls were on Vaccarès opposite Carralet. Here I spent a deal of time on the arids, looking at the larks. Cresteds were numerous, and skylarks only slightly less so. Here I saw one short-toed lark. My views of it were perhaps not quite as good as I should have liked for absolute certainty, but I feel confident the identification was correct.

This is a good small bird country. Spectacled warblers were abundant, and ashy-headed wagtails conspicuous. I have yet to see a true blue-headed wagtail; all that I have critically examined have poor eye stripes and white throats and are therefore *cinereocapilla* and not *flava*. But the latter must be a common migrant, I should imagine. This Carralet ground looked excellent for tawny pipit, but I saw none.

'Smelly Alley' was at its worst. More dead carp were in the first stages of decomposition, which must be a rapid process in this heat. Their aroma was beyond a joke. But we burst through the gassed area and made for the stilts without delay. They were still there in the pool, but more of them. Three pairs were wading in the shallow water and another couple were stalking about on the arids amongst the *Salicornia*. They were as noisy as ever when we drew near, but as all eight of them, both cocks and hens, retired to the water and began feeding, I realized that they were not yet incubating. Clearly, however, this is to be a breeding place this year, and I fondly hope that they will hurry up about it, for there are only five days left.

It was while I was watching the pair of stilts in the *Salicornia* that I made the discovery. My glass lighted on a number of creatures which for a moment, ridiculous as it may sound, I thought were weasels. Then I saw—pratincoles, and at least thirty of them! Here again there are only two records that I can find for this species for the Camargue.[1] What lay in front of me

[1] Mayaud (1938) summarizes the known facts about this species in the Camargue. Apparently it was a nesting bird in the last century, and Mon. Hugues, who was for a while responsible for the bird notes in the *Actes*, says that it is a nesting species in the Crau and Camargue, but he gives no details. Mayaud adds, 'It would be good to get exact data on the actual nesting of the pratincole.' In view of this I might add to my own record the discovery of a colony by my friend W. B. Alexander near Méjeanne in 1938—possibly the same as mine, for the Canal Michel ground was deserted in 1938, and Méjanne is only some two miles to the north of it.

was clearly a colony—and at this season it must surely be for nesting purposes.

Excited as I was, I had a good look at them on the ground. Once again I was impressed by that strange dreamy look which is created by the black V which runs down from the eye to the throat and encloses within it a patch of cream-yellow. I was close enough, too, to see that the base of the bill is red. As in Spain they reminded me in their stance of Arctic skuas and in the air, too, when they are also very tern-like. Certainly one could not connect this strange bird with the plovers. When I inspected the ground, they rose in alarm and circled round me calling without ceasing. I hunted high and low but failed to find a nest. All the same I cannot believe that they do not propose to settle here.

With that we called it a day—and not a bad one either.

MAY 5TH. The curse is upon us again. After days of halcyon weather the mistral has returned. Being just at the end of our stay, it is heart-breaking, for photography in it is out of the question. Thank goodness some of our hides have been taken in, but those on the hoopoe and fantail are still out. I doubt if they are still standing despite the multitude of guys which peg them down.

Forgetting our cameras we once more did the circular tour round Les Saintes Maries and Badon. There have been a remarkable number of flamingoes about all day, so many that it seems incredible that they should be proved to nest in the delta so rarely. For what purpose then are these great numbers here during the summer? One herd to-day we actually saw inland, on a small pool in the arids round the Étang de Consecanière—a testimony to the violence of the gale which alone will drive them off their beloved lagoons. Impérial was full of them—so too was Fangassier. Where they have been during the early part of our stay I cannot think. They seem to have appeared from nowhere.

We have recorded, however, a few new species—for us. Impérial provided us with a carrion crow (flying over), three dunlin, a black tern, and a trip of grey plover. On the return journey we called in at the third reserve of the Société d'Acclimatation—L'Avignolle. It is sited on the eastern shores of Fangassier, and we ventured far over the muds. Here the far-flung landscape is more like the saltings of the Wash than anywhere I have seen in the Camargue. We had hoped for avocets. They were present, but not breeding yet, I fear. Out on the *étang* we saw eight widgeon—a late date for them, and as I was stumbling back through the *Salicornia* I flushed a Kentish plover from three eggs. This nest was remarkable for its cover, as may be imagined from the fact that I flushed her like a snipe at my feet, so deeply buried in the scrub was she—a marked contrast to the open sites we have hitherto seen. Little terns were also numerous, especially off the islets in the *étang*. On the way back, at Villeneuve, we saw the first spotted flycatcher. It has most decidedly not been one of our better days!

MAY 6TH. The mistral again at its worst—gale force. We spent the morning on the pratincole ground. This time we subjected it to a very thorough search, and we were rewarded by finding four nests—two with two eggs apiece and two with one. Laying is clearly only just beginning, for there were many scrapes as yet unlaid in. This is all very exciting, for it is apparently the first definite breeding record for the Camargue. Indeed, so far from nesting even the bird itself is a rarity. Glegg only gives two records for the species, and Tallon whom I told to-night knows of no previous occurrence of nesting, though the bird has apparnetly been seen by him since Glegg's list near Giraud. Certainly the country is well suited to their requirements, and it is a bird one would expect—especially in view of the extensive stony desert just east of the Grand Rhône—the Crau, which we have not yet visited, but which from all accounts sounds an ideal place.

The nests are the merest scrapes in the baked and cracked mud, and most of them are sheltered by the smallest of *Salicornia* bushes. The eggs are lovely, spherical and not pyriform like most waders' eggs. Creamish in ground colour, they are handsomely blotched with lilac and brown. Oh that the mistral drops in time to give me a chance to get at the parents with my camera!

The *garde* of the estate, however, has had other views, for he came up to-day to see what we were about. Apparently the owner of the shooting lives in Marseilles. So at lunch time to-day

PLATE 38. BLACK-WINGED STILT (MALE) ABOUT TO INCUBATE EGGS

PLATE 39. BLACK-WINGED STILTS—FEMALE ABOUT TO RELIEVE MALE

PLATE 40. BLACK-WINGED STILTS—MALE ABOUT TO RELIEVE FEMALE

PLATE 41. BLACK-WINGED STILTS ON NESTING GROUND—FEMALE SITTING; MALE ON GUARD

we wired him and to-night, bless his heart, he has given us permission to get to work. When I came out here, I fondly thought that my permits from the Société d'Acclimatation would carry me anywhere. Actually they cover quite a small area, and much excellent ground lies without their law, as for instance this pratincole and stilt country—and the egretry.

The four pairs of stilts were still about the place, and judging from the way they joined the pratincoles in flying round they must be very near laying, although they seem more interested in the arids than in the pool—which surprises me, if indeed they are going to nest here. On the pool to-day was a pair of gadwall.

The necessity of wiring to Marseilles took us home for lunch, and the fury of the mistral discouraged us from returning into the Camargue. Instead, we became good tourists again and visited the magnificent walled town of Aigues-Mortes. The trip produced two birds we had not hitherto seen in Provence. A fine cock Montagu's harrier, resplendent in his grey blues and blacks, was quartering a field. It is strange that we have seen so little of this species, for marsh harriers have by now become like sparrows in our eyes!

Near Aigues-Mortes itself a strange bird of prey was perched on the telegraph wires. At first I thought it was a hobby, of which species we have recently seen a number on passage, but as soon as the glasses were on it, that identification was found false. In fact, I cannot identify the bird. It is a new one on me. Fortunately it was very obliging, and I sat down on the running board of the car and noted its plumage in detail. They were as follows: back, brown and barred; head, pinkish brown with a very light forehead indeed; face, white with a small hobby-like moustache; breast, buff with light brown flecks; legs, orange. I saw it so well and have so clear a picture of it that it should be easy to give it a name when I can get at some skins.[1]

MAY 7TH. The gods be praised! The mistral has dropped. It is indeed a kind concession from fate. P. started the day with a session on the hoopoe. While I was putting him into the hide a pair of large raptors sailed over. They were *probably* Bonelli's

[1] Mr. B. W. Tucker kindly identified it for me from my description as a female red-footed falcon, probably immature.

eagles, for this species is known to visit the egretry during the summer months—but they were too high for certain identification. Not proven.

Thence to see what we could make of the pratincoles. At Méjeanne we had a glorious view of a cock golden oriole, a blaze of the most brilliant yellow. Really, the golden oriole is yellow beyond belief. It is not often that one cannot find some subject of everyday life with which to compare a bird colour, but the brilliance of the oriole is past comparison. Just as the blue of the kingfisher is beyond description, so too are the oriole's yellows.

At Carralet, our old friend, the grey heron, was again fishing. Nearer the Canal Michel a small party of black terns were hovering over a dyke liberally grown with water crowfoot. They looked truly lovely, their black contrasting with the white carpet over which they hovered.

Up 'Smelly Alley' we found the carp-catcher at work, busy with his nets. Intrigued, we stopped to watch. His haul was astonishing. His nets oozed eels and great fat carp. From a small drain such as this is it was the more surprising. I asked the fisherman if he hauled his nets regularly. He replied, 'Every day all the year.' But where do the carp come from in such quantity? Surely they cannot stand such a deadly holocaust *every* day? We retired mystified.

On the pratincole ground we found some clutches increased to three, and located several more nests. The birds were skimming about, backwards and forwards and around us, so fast that a count was impossible, but I think my original estimate of fifteen pairs about right. By now, too, we must have found quite seven or eight nests.

I put a hide up at some considerable distance from one just to watch the bird back. I had not been in it for ten minutes before my attention became concentrated on a lone stilt striding elegantly and fast through the *Salicornia*. To my joy I saw it gingerly lower itself on to eggs. I signalled P. who relieved me from my hide. Inspection revealed a nest, set in a small bed of sea lavender, and it contained four lovely eggs. The site interests me. From mere book learning I had always associated stilts with water. Yet here this pair is nesting in a desert of hard-baked mud which it shares with the pratincoles. In fact, it is in the middle of their colony. The pool where we first saw them is at least two hundred yards off. A bird will always refute you if it can!

We soon had a hide up, at some considerable distance, and we spent the rest of the day in moving it up to within working distance, checking up between each stage to see that the stilt accepted it. On each occasion she went straight back without so much as a glance at the strange erection. It might never have been there! I believe she would have let us work her straight off!

While we were doing this, I found a lapwing's nest with a clutch of four, and also a single chick. Truly this little 'field' is full of birds. In between hide shifts we wandered over into the Marais de la Sigoulette. I shall always remember the huge flock of drake red-crested pochards which rose from its edges. They are the finest duck I know, and that is saying much in this handsome family. The marsh teemed with birds. Purple herons were particularly abundant. Has any bird of this size so slender a neck? Marsh harriers swarmed over the reeds. Whiskered terns are also clearly going to use this *marais* for nesting. A number were flying over and around all day, calling harshly. I could spend a whole summer in a square mile round here with ease and delight!

MAY 8TH. I have to-day redeemed a vow. Ever since I first saw a stilt wading sedately in the salt mines at Cadiz I have promised myself the pleasure of sitting near this lovely creature. To-day that dream has been realized. And what a realization! Even had I had power to command a bird to act, it could not have played its part better! But let events speak for themselves.

P. opened on her with his ciné camera. I was to give him two hours, unless he signalled earlier with his handkerchief out of the back of the hide. Twenty minutes later I saw it appear. Wondering what had gone wrong, I ran the gauntlet of 'Smelly Alley' to the hide. 'What's the matter?' 'Matter? I've got all I want. Never seen a bird like it. Not only the hen, but the cock has been present at the nest all the time!' It sounded well. We moved the hide considerably closer, and I got in.

It was as P. had said. No sooner was he out of the field than both birds began a positive race for the eggs. The hen won, and settled down. The cock—angry?—came up to her. She crooned

gently. He stalked off. He came up behind her. She still refused
to move. He bent his stilts and gently prodded her with his beak.
At this she rose. He incubated, his wife standing beside him.
Five minutes later she demanded a turn. He gave place. And so
it went on—an unending record of nest-reliefs. I have never seen
two birds like it. They lived in each other's pockets. Both birds
were within, at the furthest, six yards of the nest the whole time.
More often than not the non-sitting bird stood over its incubating partner.

Explanations of such behaviour are impossible. Was it due to
the heat of the ground? The mud was so hot that it hurt the hand
to touch it. I can think of no other reason for such odd behaviour
—but it suited my book very nicely. From the word 'go' neither
stilt so much as looked at the hide except casually. Even at seven
feet they ignored it and the noises from within, so much were
they wrapped up in one another.

I shall never forget to-day—the loveliness of their white
bodies and black wings, the elegance of their quick high-stepping
strides, the charming understanding between those two birds,
their low croons to one another. Little, O birds, do you
know what pleasure you have given to the inmate of that stuffy
tent!

I ramble—and who would not? I was much intrigued to
watch how this high-standing bird got its body down from its
pedestal on to the eggs. It is a pretty sight. On arriving at the
nest the head is lowered and the eggs inspected, as though it
were measuring the distance of its descent. Calculations made,
the red stilts are slowly bent at the 'knee' and the bird gradually
lowers itself. The breast first makes contact. In this position the
tail sticks at an acute angle into the air, then come the wing tips
and finally the 'knees'. From this posture it shimmies on to the
eggs, the tail waggling in the process. Then, slowly again, it
lowers its extremities until tail and wings fall into their normal
place. Thus fixed, it levers itself up very slightly, and, its balance
gained, finally shuffles on, when its red 'knees' protrude far
behind. I have tried to take a series of photographs of each stage
in this performance, but only P.'s ciné will really do justice to its
grace. O you lovely bird! Yet Buffon thought from his examination of skins that the stilt was an example of nature at fault.

PLATE 42. BLACK-WINGED STILTS ON NESTING GROUND—MALE SITTING; FEMALE ON GUARD

PLATE 43. NEST AND EGGS OF PRATINCOLE

PLATE 44. NEST AND EGGS OF KENTISH PLOVER

Dead, stuffed atrocities may give this impression. How quickly does the living bird dispel it!

In the course of our many comings and goings over this ground I found yet another pratincole's nest, and also, hidden at the foot of a *Salicornia* bush, an ashy-headed wagtail's with one egg—which only serves to emphasize what I felt yesterday, that I would with pleasure confine myself to this area for the rest of the summer—despite the heat, and judging by to-day's temperature, I hesitate to think what it must be like in June!

By lunch time I had exposed four dozen plates and P. many feet of film. We transferred the hide on to a pratincole and went off to La Capelière to see if our spectacled warbler of April the 26th had hatched. Fortune again was with us. All four chicks were out of their shells and approximately twenty-four hours old —certainly not more and probably less. According to Bouisset, when we found her on the 26th, she was just sitting, for he had seen both birds about on the 24th. Thus the incubation period for this species would seem to be between thirteen and fourteen days. When flushed from the nest, the hen gave an elaborate display of injury feigning. She scuttled over the mud amongst the *Salicornia* with wings fluttering piteously and with her head hung limply down. Here again we erected a hide, this time almost on the road itself, but safe enough, for Bouisset can watch it for us. When we had checked up to see that she had returned to her chicks, we returned to Arles. To-morrow, our last day in the Camargue, we hope to get both pratincole and spectacled warbler. If the mistral rises . . . !

MAY 9TH. A day of feverish activity. We have worked from dawn to dewy eve, not only inside hides but also dismantling some, and widespread they were. The egretry, La Capelière, the Canal Michel, Villeneuve—all are now packed away. Would it were not so, and that we had another month in this paradise!

P. started on the hoopoe. From the faint noises issuing from within he deduces that she has chicks. In the meantime I visited my pratincole. The eggs were warm; she had been sitting overnight. It looked promising. But a long session failed to reveal her. Indeed, only a mere sprinkling of the colony was present at all.

The rest had vanished into thin air. But I noticed one bird sitting studiously. The hide was transferred to her nest, and I determined to sit it out on her later in the day.

In the course of these manœuvres I found another stilt with three eggs and yet another lapwing with clutch four. Our total of nests for this small arid area now numbers thirteen—eight pratincoles, two stilts, two lapwings, one ashy-headed wagtail. In addition there is certainly a stone curlew breeding here. I have heard the birds calling as danger approaches. All this in an area of two hundred square yards, if as much!

We left the pratincole to get used to the hide, and went off to La Capelière, where the spectacled warbler behaved like a book. Both birds were feeding and at frequent intervals, and both were most punctilious about removing excreta from the nest. This they carried away in their beaks. There was no injury-feigning display to-day. My plumage notes of the cock from the hide run as follows: crown, bluish grey; back, dull brown; wings, a rich red-brown; throat, white shading gradually into a breast very softly suffused with pink. At close quarters the 'spectacles' round the eyes were conspicuous—though at a distance they are not a good character. The female colour scheme follows the same lines, but is more subdued in all respects. She lacks particularly the blue-grey crown of her lord. Once again I came away with the impression of a whitethroat rather than a Dartford warbler, and if there is to be confusion, it should be with the former rather than the latter.

We said good-bye to Bouisset with regret and returned to the pratincoles. The bird was sitting. Once again I was hopeful, but in five hours I saw never a sign of her. Frankly I am completely mystified by the behaviour of this species. During these hours the *whole* colony would simply vanish into thin air. Heaven knows where they went! An hour or so later all would come screeching over, and for a few minutes the air would ring with the calls of flying birds. Perhaps one or two would settle for a moment. Then again they vanished into the blue. Two hours later back they came! And so it went on. I feel sure this performance had nothing to do with the presence of the hide. Many of the nests were a good hundred and fifty yards away, and they were as continually neglected as my own. The truth probably is that incubation has not started in earnest. In any case the heat of the mud would hatch any egg![1]

And so regretfully I had to give the pratincoles best. It has been a great disappointment. Thence across to Tourtoulen to dismantle the egret hide—a depressing job. En route near Villeneuve we saw another little owl and a female Montagu's harrier, the first we have seen within the strict boundaries of the Camargue. In the egret swamp I climbed to one night heron which had chicks. They are clearly earlier breeders than their white cousins. The irritating wood wrens with the half-songs were still present in numbers. As we carted the hide material back to the car, Cetti's warbler bombarded us with song. To my ears—for I have yet to see the singer adequately—it had a ring of derision about it. It threw out a challenge. Perhaps next year . . . for to-morrow we go north.

[1] When writing this I had not read of Mr. Bently Beetham's similar experience with this species in the *marismas*. See his chapter on the pratincole in his *Among Our Banished Birds*. Apparently this vanishing trick is a characteristic of the bird.

A PROVENCE DIARY

THE CAMARGUE—THE CRAU—THE CHAINE DES ALPILLES

H

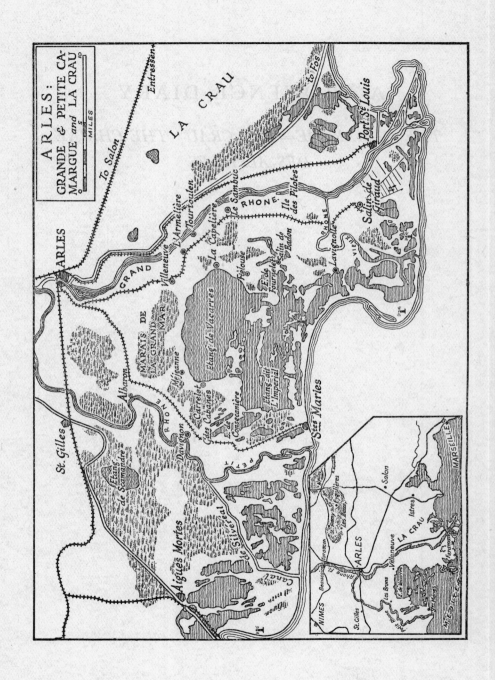

ARLES: GRANDE & PETITE CA-MARGUE and LA CRAU

A PROVENCE DIARY

THE CAMARGUE—THE CRAU—THE CHAINE
DES ALPILLES

APRIL 13TH. The Camargue again—and the mistral! Although, apart from the night herons, the main object of my return is to explore the Crau and the Alpilles, I spent this morning in the happy task of renewing old acquaintances, both human and territorial, in the delta. Is there any human experience better than the re-visiting of spots sacred to the memory? This is where we first watched a flamingo, there a purple heron, and so forth. To others it means nothing, but to him whom it personally touches it is the very breath of life. Just so have we spent to-day, even to the extent of taking our 'elevenses' with old Bouisset, who with Madame is as fit as ever.

Yet what a difference to-day confronted our eyes! As I already knew from Tallon's correspondence, the winter has been exceptionally dry, and, although I was prepared for a general lowering of the water level, the actual fact itself is beyond my worst expectations. In the Tête de la Camargue, as we sped through, no change can be noted. But Vaccarès presents a sad scene. Where last year the water of the *étang* plashed against the side of the road, now half to three-quarters of a mile of hard-baked mud separates the lagoon edge from its border. Fresh *marais* which last year had held water above the level of thigh waders are bone dry, and dead dried reeds crackled under foot. Even the drains hold only a trickle.

Upon the bird life this metamorphosis has naturally reacted most unfavourably. In the morning, for instance, we saw only sixteen different species against forty-four on last year's first day. Even with allowance for the fortnight's difference in date this great drop tells its own story. It remains to be seen if the drought

[115]

has merely concentrated the many aquatic species in the few localities which are still favoured with water. Under similar conditions in the *marismas* in 1935 that had undoubtedly happened. Perhaps in time with further exploration we shall find it to be the case here.

Yet the change is not without interest, for while it has reduced certain species, it has seemingly not touched others which at first sight one would imagine would be the first to remove themselves to better watered climes. Flamingoes, for instance, are here in undoubtedly greater numbers than last year. The northern shores of Vaccarès—the sheltered bays—were packed with them. They were present in the corner where last year I stalked and photographed them, and they stretched in a long thin pink line right round, vanishing in a pink haze over by Carrelet. Yet I should have thought that the flamingo would have been amongst the first of birds to depart.

The other side of the picture can best be told in two bare facts. We saw not a single purple heron *and only one egret*! Last year the thin, attenuated forms of the first had everywhere jumped from the roadside dykes, especially between La Capelière and Badon. To-day not one. Naturally the contrast is the more noticeable in the case of the egrets, for on our last visit their pure white silhouettes against the blue sky had been so much a feature of the Camargue that it seems a different place without them.

Nor have I to-day seen any Kentish plovers, and no terns, only a single black-headed gull. But the marsh harriers were quartering the ground in their usual numbers. They do not seem to mind. We also saw a Montagu, which species last year we found only on our last day.

There is little change to report in the birds of the arids. Corn buntings are their usual ubiquitous selves; the magpies still dominate the scene; goldfinches are still numerous and the wild flocks of house sparrows, so different from our cheeky birds, are round the farms. We saw a hoopoe, a green woodpecker, a few kestrels, many swallows, and that completes the list save for a penduline tit at La Capelière, and a linnet which was defying the mistral's cold by building its nest. The stonechats are gone; the spectacled warblers were not seen—but perhaps the mistral

PLATE 45. NEST AND EGGS OF BLACK-WINGED STILT

PLATE 46. NEST AND EGGS OF PURPLE HERON

PLATE 48. SUBALPINE WARBLER

PLATE 47. SUBALPINE WARBLER

has put them down. Ashy-headed wagtails, so conspicuous last April, were now equally conspicuous by their absence—but again perhaps they have not yet arrived.

In short, the Camargue is far from being the paradise it was last year. On the other hand, it will be interesting to see if the new conditions favour the birds of the arids. Will stone curlew and pratincoles be numerous? Perhaps—we shall see.

It was therefore with a feeling of foreboding that we turned again towards Tourtoulen and the old egretry, for it is especially to work night herons that I have come. Yet if the comparatively small drop in water level last season had been sufficient to cause the great Pilotes colony to be deserted, what chance was there that the Tourtoulen one would not also be abandoned? I seem to specialize in trying to work deserted heronries!

As we walked along the old bank of the Rhône, not a sound issued from the depths of the trees which last year had been a squawking mass of a myriad egrets. No white crosses flashed gleaming against the sky. The place was dead. We plunged in, hacking our way through the dense undergrowth. In the part where the dabchicks' nests of last April had floated over three feet of water the ground was dry, and we wandered in shoes over the old branches and boughs which a year before had tangled our feet as we plodded laboriously through the flood in thigh waders. It was a scene of desolation. Again I felt I was in a cemetery. I had known this place before as one of ceaseless activity, of constant comings and goings, of much guttural chattering. Now it was silent, dead.

And then we heard them—quite suddenly, and since we had been in the colony for no little while, most surprisingly. From one tree a night heron squawked and heavily fluttered into the top branches of its tree, where it swayed its thick-set neck at us. Then another became alarmed, and after that more. This encouragement lent wings to our efforts, and soon it was apparent that there were a few pairs—perhaps thirty, but as yet it is only a guess. And, the gods be praised, they are breeding, for I found a broken egg beneath an alder, although I saw no nests with eggs amongst those to which I climbed. But I did not purposely disturb the birds very much. Breeding is clearly only just beginning, and close examination can wait. The relief of this discovery was great, for this re-visit to the Camargue we have made expressly to get the better of *Nycticorax*.

Yet, if the night herons are our primary object, the birds of the Crau and the Alpilles have loomed large in our expectations. It was to a preliminary examination of the first of these that we addressed ourselves this afternoon. Last year pressure of work in the Camargue itself had prevented us from working this strange area, for the Crau defies description. In England it can only be compared to the stony flats of Dungeness, but such a comparison implies only a portion of the truth.

The Crau lies in a triangle between Arles, Salon, and Fos. It begins, at the Mas des Pernes, in a wilderness of prickly bushes which grow seemingly out of the very stones themselves. These in time, as though reluctant to continue the struggle, dwindle away, and after a few brave olive groves finally give place to the bare open desert—the Plain of Hercules. It is a land of mirage, a flat expanse of nothingness. One word describes the Crau—stones. Stones unto stones! They stretch away as far as the eye can see, until lost in the mirage of the horizon. Over them wander flocks of sheep that eke a living out of nothing. Poor beasts, they must roll the very stones in their mouths to suck off what vegetation clings to them! Their scraggy bodies tell a clear story of want and lack of sustenance. No white sheep these, but drab and dirty as the desert they frequent, yet carefully tended always by a shepherd.

It is a land at first forbidding, but, as time passes, it casts its spell upon you, until you feel that true indeed is the fable how that Zeus made this desolation to save from his enemies great Hercules, attacked as he returned triumphant from Iberia with the heifers of Geryon. It is a pretty story, and one that fits the spirit of the place better than mere geological explanation.

Over its flat barrenness the mistral tore with unimpeded fury, so powerful that even little stones were rolled along like autumn leaves in a sudden gust. Never have I felt a wind so strong. It rent against the car; it rocked it from side to side; it whistled through the long straight avenue of telegraph wires; it blew as though the devil himself were in its tail. Not, as may be imagined, the best of days for bird watching!

We began, however, in the comparative shelter of the Mas des

Pernes, where the thick wilderness of scrub protected us from the real violence of the mistral. This country would, I hoped, prove a habitat for the South European grey shrike, which is said to breed in the Crau. It looked just right, but I saw none in a long search. Indeed, I saw only four species in this extensive thicket—red-legged partridge, magpie, subalpine and Sardinian warblers. Of the first of these warblers I got but the merest glimpses as they skulked in the undergrowth, enough for identification (the white moustaches), but never a view that satisfied. On such a day one could not expect cover-loving warblers to be sitting on their singing perches.

With the Sardinian I was more lucky. I heard him first of all—a typical whitethroat-like song. And then I saw him singing, delivering his set piece in short jerky bursts as he fluttered weakly from bush to bush. Then, in the kindness of his heart, he sat perched in full view, so close that glasses were almost unnecessary.

The cock Sardinian is a very handsome blackcap. But the black of the crown is deeper, I think, and the contrasts with the surrounding plumage are stronger, for it is sharply demarcated by the soft greys of the nape and back, and it is thrown up against the white of the throat and underparts. Above all, the black comes *beneath* the eye. My mind went back to my Spanish orphean warblers in which the black of the head also comes below the eye, but this Sardinian cannot be confused with them, for in orphean the cap merges gradually into a brown back, and there is no marked contrast with the greys and whites. Besides, orphean is a bigger bird—and looks it. Even were this not enough, the eye is . . . well, an eye opener. I stood fascinated. The brown iris glared at me through a ring of brilliant red. It dominated the whole bird: it suppressed into insignificance all other features.

The hen, too, joined the identification parade. Beside her lord she was a subdued creature. Her 'black' head was almost brown: she had no clear, clean greys; no pure white underparts. Above all, she had no fiery eye. She appeared with a bent in her beak, so I settled down to watch. Later the cock also carried some nesting material into a prickly bush. Apparently then both sexes help to build the nest. I searched hard, but failed to find it, and not wishing to disturb them so early in their operations, I left its discovery till a later day—at least I hope so.

In the real Crau, the land of a myriad stones and scraggy sheep, the wind made satisfactory bird watching impossible. I braved the elements for a few minutes, but a short walk across the desert was sufficient to show that this for all its inhospitable nature sheltered—though that is hardly the right word—countless larks. Skylarks were abundant; cresteds rather local; but short-toed predominated. Even the gale did not damp these hardy little larks. I like the short-toed's song. It may not be so elaborate as our own bird's, but it has a series of pleasant little notes of great musical quality. I like too its song flight, for the short-toed does not sing as it mounts in ever-heightening spirals. It gains its pitch, and here it dips up and down, the sweetest notes coming on the downward swoop.

Further down the Fos road at Retour des Aires we turned in to some tumbledown barns which the map calls Brunes d'Arles. We were now right in the middle of the wilderness, and here the short-toed larks were in great abundance. One was but a few feet from the car, and of it, for a moment in the shelter of one of the barns, I got a first-class view. It struck me as being more strongly marked than in the case of the Spanish birds I remember. The eye stripe and wing markings in particular showed up well. At the same time these contrast with the white underparts. At such close quarters I saw admirably the two darkish patches on either side of the throat. These diagnostic characters are by no means too easy to see at a distance. Often the wind will ruffle a skylark's plumage and expose the darker under-feathering, giving just this impression, so that care must be taken.

APRIL 14TH. The mistral drove all thoughts of Camargue and Crau from our minds, and we thought that we might stand a better chance of survival, if we visited the Alpilles, for surely somewhere in the hills there would be shelter. So we turned the car north to the high ground some fifteen miles away.

As one approaches Les Baux up the winding road which leads from the olive groves of the valley, the Alpilles loom up on either side—sierra-like in their jagged points and foothills of loose rock and scrub. A nearer view shows that they are made up of many

PLATE 49. BITTERN

PLATE 50. FANTAIL WARBLER REMOVING FAECES FROM NEST

PLATE 52. FANTAIL WARBLER APPROACHING NEST

PLATE 51. FANTAIL WARBLER EMERGING FROM NEST

PLATE 53. THE CRAU—STONES AND SHEEP

Short-toed Larks are the characteristic birds of such ground. Crested and Skylarks are also common with an occasional Black-eared Wheatear. A few Pintail Sand-Grouse also occur

PLATE 54. SCARCE SWALLOW-TAIL BUTTERFLY (*GRAPHIUM PODALIRIUS*)

small points of rock scarred and pitted into strange patterns. Here and there along the higher ground are rugged crags, which assume ghoulish shapes.

The Alpilles indeed are nature's sculpture studio, for here she has excelled herself in drawing in stone strange figures and throwing up to heaven jagged points of rock, needles in their sharpness. What weather, time and geology have left undone, man has completed—round Les Baux itself, at least. Here into the rock face he has cut deep fissures mining out the stone, great holes in the rock like the naves of cathedrals.

The Alpilles are of outstanding fascination, with the hill town of Les Baux not the least of its surprises. From its summit one looks away over the olive groves and vineyards of the plain of Provence beyond Arles over Camargue, beyond Salon over Crau, until the eye is lost in the hazy distance where the blue Mediterranean makes contact with the land.

We parked the car near Les Baux and struck up a defile which cut a deep fissure into the hills. For a while our track carried us through olive groves reclaimed from the prevailing scrub. Here chaffinches were common and three jays were seen. Higher up woodlarks were singing in fine style and were surprisingly abundant. When this semi-cultivation ceased, the track gave out, and we found ourselves in a valley which was covered in one dense mass with cistus, dwarf gorse, and stubborn prickly scrub—a loathsome obstacle to progress, which cuts mercilessly through breeches and stockings.

This valley was the home of many Dartford warblers. Despite the force of wind which to our indignation penetrated even here, I have never seen this species sit up so well. My memories of windy days on Surrey and Dorset heaths bring back another tale —of birds which skulked in the undergrowth and would not perch. Here to-day the cock birds were flinging themselves into the air and warbling forth their typical songs, perching again as perkily as only a Dartford can, tiny mites with tails cocked up at an impertinent angle as though daring the world for all their size. We hunted hard in this valley, but it was apparently confined to Dartfords. We saw no Sardinians, nor subalpines.

From here we ran up to Les Baux itself and struck off on the slopes above the village. From the top of a lone conifer by the

[121]

road I was attracted by a thin, but very varied and not un-pleasing, little song. My glasses revealed a serin—a delightful little finch resplendent in bright yellows on the breast and head and with a brown-marked back. As I was watching him, he leapt into the air, singing mightily. This song flight reminds me much of that of a spotted flycatcher catching insects. The bird throws itself high up and with rapidly fluttering wings planes down again either to its original perch or, more often, to another—but I like him best when at the peak of his upward flight he turns about and comes fluttering back to the perch he has just left. There were a number of pairs in the immediate neighbourhood, but none, so far as I could see, outside it.

On the rocks above, just by the village itself, were a pair of blue rock thrushes—the species for which I was particularly seeking in the Alpilles. I had been told to look out for a big blackbird, and while the description serves as a general guide in so far as that is the fleeting impression one gets, yet it does little justice to this lovely bird when a good view is obtained. But they are shy and wary, and are intolerant of humanity. I chased the cock far to-day across the rocks, but there are so many nooks and crannies that the odds lie with the bird, and eventually he beat me . . . but not before I had seen him well for several minutes. What an insult to think of him as black! His body is the deepest blue-black up to the nape and throat. The rest of him is a gor-geous blue, intermediate in tone between Oxford and Cam-bridge, much the same in fact as the head of the true rock thrush which I saw last year in the Camargue. I much prefer this species to the gaudily attired other bird.

Working up to the higher ground, I again found more Dart-ford warblers. Thence I worked with much discomfort through the rough scrub down to the road. Here the Dartfords were replaced by an occasional Sardinian warbler, and side by side with these a number of subalpines. As on the Crau I found them difficult to see to advantage, but at last I not only got beautiful views but saw the display of the cock before the hen. The cock well repays the trouble necessary to observe him. The soft greys which predominate in the plumage of the head and back are separated from the orange pink of the throat and breast by a pronounced white moustachial streak. This character is most con-

spicuous and diagnostic, for only in one other European warbler
—Ruppell's—is it present, and in that bird it separates a black
head from a black throat.

In display, which took place in the cover of the scrub and only
a few feet from me, the cock makes conspicuous use of the attractive black and white pattern on the underside of his tail. This in
posturing he keeps cocked up in the attitude of a blackbird
alighting and it is fanned open to full stretch, so that the white
outer tail feathers are shown to full advantage. Thus, with shim-
mering wings, he moves about the female. She is only a slightly
duller edition of himself, rather browner of back and with perhaps less brilliant throat, but not nearly so dull as I had been led
to believe.

From Les Baux we did a round through the Alpilles to St.
Remy and back by Mausanne. The Alpilles on their northern
slopes are thickly wooded with conifers—attractive country, but
to my surprise, except for a buzzard, there were no raptors
circling over these forests. Indeed, the only bird of note was an
Alpine swift whose white belly afar proclaimed its identity.
When it raced over, it seemed very brown on top, but much
lighter than our bird, and it was close enough to see the brown-
ish band across the breast.

APRIL 15TH. During the morning we did the old circular tour of
the Camargue. The dryness is quite extraordinary. Everywhere
it is like a desert. The Canal Michel is quite dried up. Heaven
knows what has happened to the carp! My old stilt place and the
Marais de la Sigoulette look as though they have not seen a drop
of water since the flood. Conecanière is gone; Impérial, too, is
but the shadow of its former self, and looks more suitable for
beating world motor speed records than for aquatic birds. To-
day we have taken the car across *étangs* which last year were deep
in water.

In these conditions the bird life is chiefly migratory or consists
of the birds of the arids. However we have to-day seen quite a
number of species. Migrants have included wryneck (two, one in
the tamarisks at the Canal Michel and another near Conecanière), redstarts, common; a few cuckoos; a single song thrush,
and one ortolan bunting, both by the Phare de Gacherol on the

[123]

south road; an odd wheatear, woodchat, and wood wren; a yellow wagtail (sub-species?).

The birds of the *landes* are reasonably up to scratch. Spectacled warblers are common; lapwing were still at the stilt ground, but no pratincoles. The land round Carrelet still swarms with larks; linnets are in the *Salicornia*. The water birds—except flamingoes —are in a sad state. In our whole round we have not seen a single purple heron and the egrets are few and far between though, to be sure, there are more on the Saintes-Maries than on the Badon side.[1] Marsh harriers at least have not suffered.

The *étangs* were sadly lacking in life. There were a few terns, but far out, and I could not identify them, an occasional herring gull and one lesser black back. A few Kentish plover ran about on the muds (where any could be found without a long trek into the *étangs*). Avocets were seen only near the Gacherolle light-house and on Fournelet. What a change from last season when they swarmed along this south road! I saw and heard a single curlew: there were scattered redshank. And that is the total except for a few mallard. Not an encouraging survey!

After lunch we went to the Crau where I spent the rest of the day in the Mas des Pernes watching Sardinians and subalpines. At least here one gets some protection from the mistral, and indeed it was not such a fruitless visit, for I found the nest of my Sardinian which I watched building two days ago. It had not yet got eggs, but was clearly completed, very whitethroat-like and built in a similar site.

APRIL 16TH. A glorious day with no mistral. We spent it in the Crau. The effect of the tranquillity on the Sardinian and sub-alpine warblers at the Mas des Pernes was a revelation. In my earlier visits to these bushes, when the wind has been at full force, only odd snatches of song from the depths of deep cover had revealed the presence of bird life. This morning, soon after sunrise, the whole place was teeming with warblers. Subalpines abounded, far outnumbering the Sardinians. They were almost different birds, so changed was their behaviour, from the wind-

---

[1] It was later proved that in this dry year (1938) the egrets nested beyond Les Saintes-Maries at the mas de Sablons in La Petite Camargue. This was apparently not a new colony, but had been occupied for some years, though hitherto unknown to a competent ornithologist.

PLATE 55. FLAMINGOES FEEDING ON THE ETANG DE VACCARES

PLATE 56. FLAMINGOES ON THE OPEN WATER

PLATE 57. FLAMINGOES IN FLIGHT (S. SPAIN)

blown, unhappy creatures that previously had skulked about the undergrowth. As if in praise to the sun, they now perched high on the bush tops and poured out a stream of attractive white-throat music. How like in ways and mannerisms these true *Sylviidae* are! It was indeed a change to be able to sit down with the telescope and watch these birds. I noted again the grey colouring of the back which contrasts so pleasingly with the pinks of the underparts, pinks that are brightest on the chin, where the white moustachial stripe divides them from the soft greys of the head.

I worked hard for a nest, for both these warblers are early breeders, but it was not to be; nor indeed was there any further progress of note at my Sardinian's nest. Yet this morning has not been wasted. I feel I now know my subalpine warbler well. So often in mere bird watching the observer comes away with the feeling that although he has seen his bird to best advantage, he is not yet intimate with it. It is a feeling that has made me rarely claim really to know a bird until I have sat within a few feet of it and watched it from a hide. I have however this morning been so much amongst subalpines that they are a very real part of my bird experience, no longer the mere scratch acquaintances and hazy impressions which so often form a bird watcher's mental picture of a species.

The open Crau of stones and sheep is clearly the province of short-toed and skylarks. To-day they were both much in evidence, as well they might be after the buffeting they have had. Everywhere larks were singing. They are indeed extraordinarily numerous. I wandered far over the wastes, but disturbed none from a nest. For the short-toed at least it is probably a little early.

Later in the day on our way home on the far side of the Crau between Entressen and the main Salon road I found calandra larks in large numbers. They seem to prefer less exposed ground than the short-toeds, for they were frequenting a stony part which had a reasonable covering of very low vegetation. I spent much time in their company, for I had never really got to know them well while in Spain—despite falling off my horse's neck into a nest!

This species is a lark with a personality. The short-toed is rather an insignificant little bird—a washed out and not very exciting skylark. The calandra is in no way so disappointing. It is distinctive not only in plumage but in song and flight. Seen on the ground, it is a big heavy dark coloured lark with black patches on the neck which are conspicuous and clear, not indecisive marks as in the short-toed. Indeed in well marked specimens—and they vary in the degree of its intensity—the black seems almost to form a V on the neck. In flight it shows much black and white, for the wing feathers are very dark indeed, and they are white-tipped.

The song and the flight in which it is uttered are both delightful. The phrasing of the notes is skylark-like only in its *joie de vivre*—very sweet and with a quaint rippling trill at its end. While giving tongue to the song part, the bird maintains a stationary position with steadily beating wings, but the jingle is often accompanied by a slow flapping flight with the wings beaten very deliberately and slowly. Remarkable as the comparison may seem, they reminded me in this flight of a short-tailed pratincole, a resemblance heightened, of course, by the facial disc effect produced by the black of the neck. Near the calandras I saw a grand cock black eared wheatear.

The calandras were actually our last bird hunt of the day, but between the subalpines and them we had covered much ground to the south—round Fos and Miramas. The stony desert of the true Crau gave place a little before Fos to an extensively bushed area, on the fringes of which we saw a stone curlew, but I was very much more interested in the heart of this scrub where on a telegraph wire I saw a South European grey shrike, for this species is one of my main objects in the Crau. It is an early breeder and by rights should be nesting now. It is a most handsome bird—dark of back and vinous below, with whites in flight which blend well into the general colour scheme. I watched it for a long time, but it was giving nothing away.

The rest of the day calls for little comment. Near Fos itself we found ourselves in marshy country again, and here I heard a fantail warbler. The drought certainly seems to have had an adverse effect on this species in the Camargue, for I have not yet seen it in localities where last year it abounded. Just before the village the road ran beside some salt pans. Here were a number of Kentish plovers and one black-winged stilt.

APRIL 17TH. In the morning we gave the Tourtoulen night heronry—for egretry now seems a misnomer—a thorough inspection. The swamp is indeed a striking change from last year, and now that I can see the sort of flotsam and jetsam of old and dead trees which then presumably we waded through and trod underfoot, the more I wonder that last April we did any work at all! In these unusually dry conditions it is distinctly depressing to see the vast number of nests lying idle in the trees, nests which I do not imagine will ever be used this year. At the same time there are definite consolations. To be able to walk dry-shod through the trees and to the nests is a great asset: to climb without great thigh waders cluttered up with climbing irons makes the labour a pleasure. Again, the whole swamp is no longer dark, fetid, and rather frightening as last year, but lighter and more airy. Nor does it buzz with mosquitoes and other insect unpleasantnesses—though the spiders' webs are still there to weave themselves round the face and to trammel up the nose.

After this morning's search I am inclined to think that there are more night herons than I thought on our first visit. Comparatively few are as yet nesting. After several climbs I saw in all five nests containing eggs: of these three held clutches of three, and two of two eggs each. Laying therefore has only just begun. On the whole, the occupied nests are high—higher, I think, than in 1937, due perhaps to the absence of the protective flood water underneath. Like our grey herons they quickly dirty their nests, and this same palish grey colour indicates their occupation. Night herons build true platforms, the tops of the nests lacking any real cup, though I notice on each a very meagre, but probably quite efficient, little rim of twigs round the edge.

By the river wall we heard a penduline tit and, for the first time this season, a nightingale. In the swamp itself the loud whistle of a golden oriole startled us, but I did not see the bird itself.

After lunch we went again to Les Baux. Apart from birding I had a good look at this most fascinating of hill villages. Built out of and amongst solid rock its narrow streets and its eyrie-like perch defy description, while the grey and curiously shaped rocks all around add greatly to its fascination. But as it was

Easter Sunday, it bore an unfortunate resemblance to Margate at a similar season!

I started by exploring some attractive high ground on the Arles side of Les Baux. Here I had an unpleasantly prickly passage through the scrub until I reached the crags—but the less said about that the better, for I had only flannels on! Never again! On top I sat down for a while out of the wind and to enjoy the sun. Two blue rock thrushes were singing amongst the boulders and scrub. In these wild surroundings the notes sounded singularly harmonious, as a ring ouzel's do on an English moor. The song bears a close resemblance to a blackbird's, save that it is slower and more emphatic in each of its phrases. I could do no more than glimpse the songsters.

At Les Baux itself the usual pair were still on their territory, despite the crowds. This blue rock thrush is nevertheless a very shy bird indeed, and in the rough ground it frequents circumstances are all in its favour. I found myself engaged in a game of hide and seek with my quarry. I emerged round a screen of rock to find him perched a few yards off. Silently he flicked away, and with great skill immediately put a boulder between himself and me. And so it went on. At last I found that I could watch him best from the road beneath his territory, for of people there he took not the least notice. He perches with all the cocksure arrogance of a male blackbird. As his feet touch his foothold, up goes his tail in that same self-assured way, and as slowly drops back into its normal position. Both birds—for his soberly coloured lady joined him—spent some time in acrobatic exercises, boomeranging up into the air like flycatchers and flicking back to earth. They *are* jolly creatures.

The serins are still active, but, considering the warmth of their sheltered cover, were not showing up as well as I thought they would. I watched a cock bird give food to his drab lady, and I spent some time in an abortive hunt for a nest. Subalpines and Sardinians were also busy in the scrub, and far away towards St. Remy were two large raptors circling over the wilder Alpilles. They were certainly not Egyptian vultures. They were therefore probably Bonelli's eagles—but not proven.

APRIL 18TH. I found P. and R. here when I rose, and so to-day

PLATE 58. SUBALPINE WARBLER

PLATE 60. SPECTACLED WARBLER (FEMALE)

PLATE 59. SPECTACLED WARBLER (MALE)

I have spent very largely playing the cicerone to them. It was not the best of days to introduce friends to the Camargue, for the mistral was at its worst. Even they, eager as they were to get on with the job, had had enough of the open delta by lunch.

We began with the night herons, for I was getting anxious to begin a hide in the tree tops. The site I have chosen out of many inspected is not too easy a place for its construction. The tree is slender and weak and not exactly overcrowded with sub-stantial branches. However, this morning I have managed to rig up a preliminary wood framework which I fondly hope will achieve its purpose, for the nest itself is well placed for photo-graphy. Having pinned up the first sack, I joined the others while my bird got back to its three eggs.

Clutches this year are small. Several birds are finally incubat-ing on two eggs; most on three; exceptionally four. Last year fours, both for egret and night heron, were the rule, while fives were common, and there was at least one six. I imagine this decrease in clutch size to be due to the arid conditions of the present season. No doubt food supplies will proportionately decline, and equally doubtless the birds know it and are accord-ingly remaining content with smaller broods.

P. and R. I found busy watching night herons. They reported a large bird which from their description could only have been Egyptian vulture—since they do not keep storks in this part of the world. We determined then to find the Rhône. Last year I had always meant to discover actually where the river was, but despite many attempts water level and undergrowth had driven me back. We ploughed on through the jungle and at last emerged on to the main stream. It is here a fine wide river, almost tropical in the luxuriance of its bank vegetation.

En route to the car I checked up on my night heron to find her sitting happily in front of the growing hide. On the river wall we saw a greenfinch and heard a coal tit. The rest of the morning was spent in showing to the others 'the ropes' round La Cape-lière and Badon. Nothing new to report—except perhaps a slight increase of egrets.

Last night Tallon in conversation had told me something about the breeding of Egyptian vultures in the Alpilles. He showed me some excellent photographs taken by Mon. de Greyling of a nest and egg and, at a later stage, with a chick. He was quite sure that de G. would be only too happy to tell me the exact locality, and he kindly armed me with a letter of introduction to him. This afternoon therefore we went across to the château at St. Etienne de Grès, where he lives. Unfortunately he was out. We heard serins in his garden and saw a grey wagtail on a stream outside.

Thereafter I spent the day in showing P. and R. the lie of the land at Les Baux and the Alpilles.

APRIL 19TH. The mistral at its worst! Indeed, even last year I cannot remember a worse day. Bird watching was really out of the question, and we would have done better sitting in a café at Arles. However, we wasted the usual dose of petrol in a visit to the Camargue.

We went first down to Badon. The flamingoes were in their serried ranks on Vaccarès and Fournelet, all of them in the sheltered bays on the lee shore. Nor do I blame them. Indeed to-day every bird we have seen has been deliberately striving to avoid the force of the gale. On Vaccarès, for instance, many mallard and a few shoveler were off the water and sitting out on the muds at its edge, just as one sees them do on the Wash flats in winter when a north-easter has made havoc of the open sea. The thought is no idle comparison, for to-day has seen a gale that would have been a wild-fowler's dream, but actually has been a bird watcher's nightmare. P. and R. started off pleased that there was a wind, thinking that it would keep them cool. They came back to-night in a *very* different mind.

It is curious how little, if any, reference, ornithological papers on the Camargue make to the mistral.[1] Yet it is so much a feature of the migration period that all discussions on that subject for this region must take it into serious account. It is a factor which cannot be ignored. At times it would force an air liner down, not to mention a wretched warbler. I am feeling particularly sore about it to-day, for it has destroyed all the fun. Blast the mistral! It is a cursed, damnable wind with not a single good point in its favour. It does not even keep you cool. Instead, it takes the skin off your nose like a banana, and it blows sand into

---

[1] The *Actes* excepted. The reports take careful note of weather conditions.

your eyes until they burn with irritation. A plague on it! May it rot at birth in its Alpine cradle.

Near La Capelière a marsh drain runs out into Vaccarès, and by the reeds and tamarisks which mark its course forms a promontory that affords shelter from the wind. Here, surprisingly, in the midst of the baked muds a little water, not yet devoured by the heat of the sun, remains. This pool has to-day been most popular. On it were a number of Kentish plover and a considerable flock of ring plovers, clearly on passage, although some were actively displaying. We scrutinized them carefully in case there should be any little ring plovers amongst them, but one and all in flight showed a white wing bar which immediately served to distinguish them as of the common species. A fine black-tailed godwit came down to this pool, nicely red on the breast. One sanderling and one greenshank completed our list of waders, though several egrets were crouching right under the tamarisk bushes of the drain's 'estuary'. They looked the height of misery with their necks tucked away into their mantles. I sympathized. A wagtail also came down to the pool. I thought it was our own yellow wagtail, which I have not seen in the Camargue, but I could not see it properly in the low vegetation. Sand martins were also present for the first time this year.

On the arids close by I got glimpses of an unhappy ortolan bunting which clearly objected to being disturbed in such conditions. When flushed, it plunged into cover as though the devil was in its tail. Not far wrong either! This species is obviously a regular April migrant in the Camargue, although Glegg's list does not mention it. It is certainly to be expected.[1]

Thence to the egretry which at least afforded some shelter. My night heron is sitting in front of the hide. I added another sack, and later checked up to see that she had accepted the addition. All was well, but after last year's experience I am taking no chances with this obviously wary bird. We heard several great tits in the nesting trees.

APRIL 20TH. The abominable mistral still! I have spent most of the day gradually working up my night-heron hide. I added a few more sacks to-day, and checked up to see that all was well.

[1] See note on page 73.

What an infernal time this tree hide building takes with a shy species! This night heron cannot pretend to have been hurried in her feelings towards the tent, for I have been careful to see that she has fully accepted each stage in its construction before advancing further. In point of fact, it is a foul tree for such activities, but beggars cannot be choosers. About twenty yards off is a second night heron's nest with two eggs. Its owner is very impatient and returns to incubate even when I am up my own tree. I wish I could get a hide up to her. It is quite out of the question, for there is nothing substantial enough at the right distance to bear my weight.

In between times we ran down to La Capelière. Near Villeneuve I got fine views of a tawny pipit. I wish all the pipits were as easy to identify as this. It is conspicuously light-coloured on the underparts with hardly a trace of any spotting. The eye stripe, too, is clean cut and beneath the eye the feathers form a brown and white combination which give it almost the impression of a moustachial streak. The view through the telescope was so good that even its flesh-coloured legs could be easily seen. If one can see the colour of a bird's legs, it may be taken for granted that it has been observed to the best advantage.

Elsewhere the migrants are clearly beginning to come in. We saw to-day the first swift, pied flycatcher and hobby, and in the Crau later on our first house martin. Otherwise, the only new birds—for this visit—have been bearded tit at La Capelière and, by Vaccarès, at last two purple herons. I do not think there is any bird I miss more than this last. A year ago they were a regular sight whenever we took the Badon road. Now . . . well, we have seen our first today. That tells its own tale.

In the evening we made a rapid visit to the Crau to inspect my Sardinian warbler. She has not yet laid, though the nest is all ready for eggs.

APRIL 22ND. Yesterday we had not the courage again to face the mistral, and accordingly gave birds a miss. To-day has been a day of tribulation. My night heron, after having accepted nearly the whole hide, has started 'jibbing' during the last stages of its construction. Mindful of this bird's timidity, I took it down. What a heart-breaking task! All our earlier work has gone for

PLATE 61. PLOUGHING IN THE CAMARGUE

PLATE 62. MARAIS DE LA GRAND MAR, CAMARGUE

PLATE 63. THE ALPILLES FROM LES BAUX

Blue Rock Thrushes are the characteristic birds of the high ground. Serins, Subalpine,
Sardinian and Dartford Warblers were common in the scrub

PLATE 64. THE ALPILLES NEAR EYGALIERES

The scrub provided a habitat for Subalpine and Sardinian Warblers, Cirl Buntings and
Jays. In the valley Woodlarks were conspicuous. The high ground is favoured by an
occasional Egyptian Vulture and Bonelli's Eagle

nothing. But better that than that we should cause a desertion. When the hide tree was again naked of its sacks, the old bird returned once more. Obstinate old devil! There is nothing for it but to give her best and leave her to bring up her brood—but unobserved, I fear, by me.

So it means beginning all over again! Nor is it so easy as that. To-day I have climbed to many nests. Yet I have not found a single one over which a hide could conceivably be constructed. The night herons are this year breeding in the flimsiest tree tops where hide building is impossible. It looks as though we are defeated. But should I later find a suitable site, I shall make the hide as small as humanly possible. This species is clearly a very nervous one and requires the most careful handling—though I fail to see how it is possible to break a bird in more gradually than the pair with which we have already failed.

The heronry was to-day ringing with those half wood wren songs which I had noted last year. There must have been a great influx of these migrants; yet not a single one delivered the full wood wren song. It is most mysterious. R. and I spent a lot of time looking at the birds through the glasses. To all intents and purposes they had all the appearance of wood warblers, but why only this half song?

At the farm at Tourtoulen I saw a long-tailed tit in exactly the same place as last year. It certainly looks as though this is a breeding place for all that there are comparatively few records for the Camargue.

What was left of the day we spent on Fournelet. En route near Villeneuve we found a field with a good number of crested larks, and we got excellent views of them. They are indeed very sandy in colour and far more 'washed-out' in appearance than the skylark. Their crests too, when raised, are pronounced, but in their normal position, lying flat along the head, they are not conspicuous. Perhaps the best general field character is provided by their marked rounded appearance when in flight.

On the *étangs* birds are showing up again to better advantage now that the mistral is of less force. Near Badon was a small flock of pintail, three fine drakes accompanied by two ducks. To our wader list for the year we added several spotted redshank and one whimbrel.

[133]

APRIL 23RD. R. and I rose early and went to the heronry. I climbed tree after tree—most exhausting. It is the same story. Try as I may I cannot find a site which affords the least opportunity for building a hide. It is all very heart- and back-breaking. Yet to-day I am no nearer success than before. Perhaps even yet in this jungle there is a site tucked away. It is only too easy to overlook an occupied nest in the tangle. But I am not sanguine. The failure of to-day's search has not improved the prospects, and there is only another week left. I feel, partly from observations of general behaviour, partly from the smallness of the clutches (many are sitting clutches of two), that breeding this year is very half-hearted. It is as though the birds sensed that the rearing of their chicks in these arid conditions is going to be a precarious and chancy business. All of which does not make my task any easier.

The heronry, however, produced a few new birds. Most surprising were a small party of about six hawfinches; a blut tit was heard; and we both saw and heard a short-toed tree creeper. Near Tourtoulen we watched a sparrow hawk chase a hoopoe, and a fine turn of speed the would-be victim showed before it took refuge in the hole of a tree. Near by an astonishing bird flashed out of a tree, across the road and out of sight. It was a fine rufus-red and very hawk-like. I have scratched my head to think what it might be, but I cannot give it a name. The view was so fleeting and unsatisfactory. I am much intrigued.

The rest of the day we spent at La Capelière. Here Cetti's warbler spat its spirited, challenging song at us. I saw a gleam of determination come into R.'s eyes, and I stood by and scoffed, informing him that Cetti was a hoax, existing only as a voice and never as a shape—for after Spain and last year here I am beginning to think Cetti a genuine *ignis fatuus*! The words were hardly out of my mouth when—wonder of wonders—the myth became reality, and, the more to make me eat my earlier words, perched on a post of B.'s garden! My eyes fairly goggled with surprise. As it was, I got the only really good sight I have ever had of this *most* elusive species.

Cetti, when it breaks cover, is an attractive little warbler. Above dark rufus predominates, contrasting sharply with the almost white belly. A pronounced light stripe runs over the eye. But it is the tail which is Cetti's most engaging feature. This is beautifully graduated and is carried perkily. In fact, I got the impression of a light-breasted wren.

Had we found nothing else all day, the fact that we had seen Cetti would alone have made it memorable. As it was, a little later we discovered another new warbler. We were inspecting the reed bed which juts out into Vaccarès opposite La Capelière when our attention was attracted to a pleasing song issuing from the midst of the reeds. The main phrases of this were very reminiscent of a sedge warbler, but they were prefaced by three or four fine notes, not unlike the introduction to a nightingale's song—*lu* . . . *lu* . . . *lu*. This I knew meant a moustached warbler, but for all my certainty it was no easy task to get a view of it. The thickness of the reed tangle which towered above our heads cut down the view to but three or four feet at a maximum. Moreover, we made a noise like a couple of elephants as we moved through that forest of dried reeds. However, the bird was fortunately so concerned with its singing that it allowed a very close approach, and for some few minutes we stood and watched it at a few feet without glasses, for the reeds made them useless.

My notes taken on the spot describe the bird as follows: crown, very dark brown, at times looking almost black; eye strip, very large and conspicuous; beneath it a pronounced dark moustache, broadening out beneath the eye; underparts, white at throat grading down to buff on the belly. I could not see much of the back. The general scheme is that of a sedge warbler, but the darkness of the crown and the conspicuous eye-stripe quickly distinguish the moustached warbler.

While we were stalking this bird, bearded tits were all round us, and about as close as our quarry itself! It is strange that we have not heard more of them before. In this reed bed at any rate they were certainly abundant, creeping up and down the reeds and taking not the least notice of us.

APRIL 24TH. A day in the Crau. It is the first I have spent in that region which has been *really* windless, and what a difference it has made to both the birds and ourselves! The fine weather of the last day or so has at last encouraged my Sardinian warbler to start using the nest which for a week now has been ready for eggs. To-day at least it contained three eggs. Not wishing to disturb the birds—though they were not present in point of fact—I merely peeped in, and I did not handle the eggs. At a casual glance they looked whitethroat-like.

We beat about the scrub at the Mas de Pernes for some time, hoping to flush a subalpine from a nest, but we found only a magpie with six eggs. This was the lowest I have yet seen—even here, where tamarisk bushes are the most favoured trees. This nest was only chest high and it occupied the whole of the top of the bush into which it was built. From the number of magpies which everywhere swarm in Provence it is a wonder to me that there is any small bird life at all. The toll which these egg thieves must take cannot fail to be very high. I heartily approve of Bouisset's 'gibbet' at La Capelière—several fruit bowls, which he keeps filled not with apples or grapes but magpies' eggs!

We then visited Entressen and the calandra lark ground. I was hoping that they might have laid, for it was earlier than this that I found a nest in Spain. The birds were very active, singing and trilling in grand style, but much wandering failed to flush a bird from a nest. Indeed I do not think that they have yet laid.

Back at the car we stopped to watch a fine cock black-eared wheatear. Close by were several short-toed larks, and others were singing up above, dipping up and down in that characteristic little song flight of theirs. Through the heat haze we saw a lark settle with a grub in its beak. It was impossible to identify the species on account of the shimmer. However, we saw it vanish into a tuft of low scrub and emerge without its food. As we went out to inspect, a pair of short-toed larks got very alarmed and called incessantly. It seemed that there must be a short-toed's nest close by. A search eventually revealed a nest with three chicks.

I spent the whole of the afternoon in a hide on this nest. All the time a pair of short-toeds were calling round me. Yet when at long last a bird eventually braved the hide and returned to the nest, it was . . . a skylark! I do not know when I have felt more disappointed. We had not seen a skylark in this neighbourhood; the short-toeds, even when I packed up, were still calling in alarm: everything had indicated that the nest belonged to them. Yet it was an undoubted skylark that returned. I did my best to make it a crested or short-toed, but I could not disbelieve the clear evidence of my eyes at six feet range! A skylark, I fear, it was, and that was that. What an anti-climax!

While we were putting up this abortive hide, we saw a flock of pintailed sandgrouse. At least I assume that that was the precise species, for it is the only one known to breed on the Crau, but our view, to say the least, was fleeting and distant. The birds were travelling like the wind—a phrase which means a deal more in this land of mistral than it does at home!

APRIL 25TH–26TH. Both yesterday and to-day I have spent in unceasing work on night heron. It is odd that those days when one has least to record in a bird diary are so often the most laborious. Yesterday morning I went down to Tourtoulen determined to climb to every nest in the colony, if need be, in a last final endeavour to discover a site on which I could build a hide. I was not sanguine, for I had combed out the heronry pretty well the other day without finding anything which gave me the ghost of a chance. But I could not fly the white flag of surrender without one more effort.

I climbed to every occupied nest I saw, and not only to the nest, but in many cases up the neighbouring trees as well, for it is in these the hide will have to be built. I toiled on and on without success. I hesitate to think how many feet of poplars and alders my climbing irons have lightly scarred. At last I had to acknowledge defeat, to my great regret, for it has been especially to photograph the night heron that I have made the journey this year.

I was making my way through the jungle to the river wall, when in a particularly thick part of the tangle I saw a night heron raise itself from a nest and peer down at me. It was one which I had not seen before, and, ironically enough, not a hundred yards from my first nest. I climbed up a neighbouring poplar to find that here at last was a possible site. A stout fork was level with the nest and about ten feet away. Between it and the bird was the top of an alder—the old, old trouble in this jungle. However, I managed to rope this obstacle out of sight, and got to work.

I found the nest at lunch time yesterday, and since then

almost without a break I have worked on the hide and on the task of accustoming the old bird to it. Time is short, and I must needs work more quickly than I should like, but I have scrupulously observed the heron's reactions to every stage of the tent's construction. If she shows the least nervousness, I shall take the lot down and give her best, as I did in the case of my first bird. In view of past experience I am making it as small as it is humanly possible for it to be. Actually, if she accepts it, it is clear that I shall never be able to take long sessions in it, for I am nearly doubled up inside. The only thing that will be comfortable will be my camera, which at least has a firm stand!

To-night I am encouraged to hope that all is going to be well, for the bird is sitting in front of a hide that is very nearly complete, and she seems quite happy. After adding each sack—and I have put them up at three-hour intervals all the time—I have sat back in the undergrowth and watched her return. She has been speedy about this, and to-night I am hopeful.

This evening, by way of variety, we visited the Mas des Pernes to 'hide' my Sardinian warbler which should have been ready— only to find the eggs gone, almost certainly eaten by a magpie. Really, I do think that the stars in their courses are being a spot hard on my labours this time!

Otherwise the two days have produced but little. How could they, since I have spent most of the time anxiously observing my night heron? However, at Tourtoulen I saw a buzzard—the first I have seen in the Camargue. And at the same place I have cleared up the mystery of the strange red 'hawk' we saw on the 23rd. I saw it again to-day, and it settled in a tamarisk bush where I got the telescope on to it. It was a cuckoo! At the time I must confess that the species had me completely defeated, but on returning to Arles I looked the matter up to find that the common cuckoo has this curious rare red variation of plumage, called the 'hepatic' variety. Such are the gaps in one's knowledge that I had never even heard of it before!

It is a most lovely bird in this plumage. The general colour scheme is that of a female kestrel, i.e. rich red brown with darker bars, and the whole of the back from head to tail is thus marked. The breast is paler brown and the belly white, barred, of course. In flight it presents a lovely rich colour. I was most fascinated and most thankful, too, to clear up the mystery of the 23rd and to close up one more chink—out of many—in my knowledge.

APRIL 27TH. R. and P. came back last night from a journey to Aigues-Mortes with an intriguing account of two raptors near St. Giles. More than that, they had put one of them off a nest which had contained one egg. From their description I put the species down as black kite.

This morning we investigated. The birds were not at the nest, for laying has clearly only just begun, but they were circling round afar off. They are undoubtedly black kites. The nest too is certainly a kite's. It is built in a tremendous poplar with the largest base I have ever seen in such a tree, and wickedly hard bark into which the irons only penetrated with the use of much force. The nest is a huge structure of twigs and has clearly been built by the birds themselves. It is lined with all the oddments of a rag and bone man's cart—string, paper, and sacking. There is still only one egg. This is most interesting, for there are no records of the species for the Camargue, and this nest is only two miles outside the official boundary of the delta.[1]

The remainder of the day I spent with my night heron. It had the impertinence to rain, and the track to Tourtoulen which had been perfectly passable in dry weather had a treacherous surface of slippery mud over which the car only managed to proceed thanks to the frequent clumps of low *Salicornia* which gave the tyres a grip. However, I was more than consoled by finding my bird sitting quite happily. I spent the rest of the day finishing the job, and watching anxiously lest she should refuse at the last moment. Bare words can convey nothing of the anxiety, of the fears and trepidations, of that last 'check up'. But once more she played up trumps, and back she came. I left her sitting. To-morrow, if the gods are kind . . . but let me count no chickens! Still, it ought to be straightforward now.

One night heron had hatched to-day. I found egg-shells under the nest and heard the chicks calling up above. As the incuba-

[1] Since writing this, I find the *Actes* give a few records for this species. It was observed in the delta from time to time between 5th April and 1st July 1935; 18th May to 28th June 1936; 20th May and 2nd June 1937. Mayaud, commenting on these records, says that they suggest nesting in the neighbourhood—which in view of my records would now seem to have been the case.

tion period is given as three weeks this would mean that the bird started sitting about April 6th, and laying soon after the 1st —which is a fortnight earlier than the authorities quote.

To-day has produced a few new species for the trip besides black kite. In the Petite Camargue we saw our first whiskered terns of the year. Here too were one or two whinchats and a whitethroat. To-night, as we sat out at our café in Arles, Scops owls were for the first time noisy, and we amused ourselves by imitating them and getting them to reply. It is a game they play well.

APRIL 28TH. How sweet is success! The more so when it is the result of much toil and labour: more still, when it comes after resignation to failure. After the 23rd I confess that I put my chances of getting photographs of night heron very low indeed. Yet to-day the great moment arrived when this shy bird was sitting on its tree-top nest with only ten feet separating it from myself.

Twenty minutes after I was left to my vigil by R. I heard the bird return to the nest tree. There on the topmost twig she perched, craning her thick-set neck from side to side inspecting the hide. Then slowly and gingerly she descended down to the fork which holds the nest. Her shy methods of approach afford a striking contrast to the indifferent hurry of the egret. She walks from bough to bough and at each stage surveys the landscape o'er before gradually lowering herself on to the nest. She looks strangely attenuated as she cautiously and gingerly stretches out her leg, lowers her head, and descends on to the next bough. Once arrived, she takes no notice of anything, but sits like a log.

The colour pattern at close quarters is simple but effective. The dark markings on the back are blue-black getting lighter on the wings: the rest of the plumage is a soft creamy-grey. There are two or three creamy plumes on the head, but these are held so close together that they look like one. The legs are pale pink or flesh coloured: the bill, blue-black, lighter at the base. But it is the eye which dominates the night heron. It is a brilliant crimson red with a black pupil. As one looks at the bird from the close quarters at which I have been with it to-day, the intensity of the eye overpowers the rest of it. It shines out like a little torch

PLATE 65. NIGHT HERON WITH NEWLY-HATCHED CHICK

PLATE 66. NIGHT HERON ABOUT TO BROOD

bulb in the dark shadows of the forest around. Not the least of the joys of bird photography is the opportunity thus given of being able to appreciate in full the wonder of birds' eyes. However close one may be outside a hide, it is never quite the same thing, for a bird is always partly lost in the greatness of the world around. But, viewed through a tiny peephole, which cuts out the environment and concentrates the whole vision on to the bird itself, there are no distractions. The view is all bird.

I spent the day thus engaged. I had to be relieved at ninety-minute intervals on account of my dreadfully cramped position which I find I cannot hold for longer together than that. However, a ten-minute leg-stretch suffices to restore the circulation, and the work goes on.

During the afternoon R. came back on one of his relief visits with the news that he had found yet another black kite's nest, just down the river wall from Tourtoulen! Once again there was no doubt about the identification or the nest, for the bird left it as we arrived, and circled round. The nest was at an appalling height up an enormous poplar that stretched into the skies. It was on a side branch which looked very slender. So I rested content with watching the bird return to it. This is all very extraordinary; two breeding records in 1938, and yet no single recorded occurrence of the species previous to this year![1] Pratincoles last year, black kite this—I wonder what new breeding species my next visit to the delta will reveal!

On our way down the river wall we found a pair of tree pipits near the farm. There are curiously few records for this bird (December 1918 and April 1931). Yet it must surely be a regular passage migrant. This pair looked as if they might even be breeding later on, but I expect they are just moving through.

APRIL 29TH. I have spent the whole day with my night heron. When we arrived at Tourtoulen, one of the black kites was circling over the car—only about fifty feet up. I hope the farmer does not see it doing this. He will probably think that it is after his chickens, and that will be the end of that. Unfortunately, nothing could be easier to shoot than this bird as it was to-day. The buzzard was also still about.

[1] See note on page 139.

I was in great hopes that I would get some activity out of my night heron, for I arrived to find her on the hatch. One chick had just emerged and was still wet. It was a funny little brown golliwog. The egg shell was beneath the tree. Another egg was chipped, and I could hear the youngster inside. But despite such a favourable moment in its breeding life I got very little action out of my stolid old bird. She came back more quickly, it is true, but she sat equally persistently and did nothing at all. Once I had high hopes: the cock came into the nesting tree. Both birds called and immediately the sitting bird ruffled up the feathers of its mantle and erected its white crown plumes. But he came no further, and eventually he retired. By the end of the day I left the old lady still brooding her one chick and the chipped egg had not yet emerged.

APRIL 30TH. My last day—and a pretty hectic one. Yesterday evening a fellow ornithologist at Arles reported finding a sub-alpine warbler's nest with chicks in the Alpilles. Would I like to see it? This morning we therefore set off early. The nest was in the middle of the wildest part of the chain between Aureille and Eygalières. The character of the Alpilles in this part is substantially the same as at the Les Baux end, but it is decidedly wilder, and there is more extensive conifer and shrub growth. As we crossed the valley up to the nesting slope, woodlarks were much in evidence near the olive groves, and scarce swallow-tail butter-flies were abundant.

The subalpine's nest was in a site which a whitethroat might well have chosen. The nest too was built on exactly the same principles. I erected a hide and got in straight away. After about twenty minutes of cursing in the undergrowth behind the cock bird came on to the nest and fed the chicks. Which done, he brooded them for a while. Then off again for food. More feeding and more brooding. So it went on. The feeding interval was about eight to ten minutes. I never saw a sign of the hen.

I confess that I am very puzzled about the female subalpine warbler. During this trip I have seen a great deal of this species both at the Mas des Pernes in the Crau, and at Les Baux, and now here at the nest. Yet, except in the case of the pair I watched courting, I have not yet seen a certain female. At least, all the

[142]

birds I have had the glasses on have been grey on the head and decidedly pinkish on the throat and breast. I have not seen any which looked dowdy or frowsy—which adjectives seem to sum up the text-book accounts of the distinction between the two sexes. In the pair I watched courting at Les Baux, the female was, side by side with her lord, certainly less bright, but I fancy that the difference would not have been at all marked unless the birds had been together for comparison. I have come to the conclusion that the *average* subalpine female is much brighter coloured than the text-books would have us believe, and that many of the birds I have thought were males have been, in fact, hens. All rather unsatisfactory, but there it is.

To-day at least the bird which has come repeatedly to the nest has been grey headed and bright orange pink at the throat and paler on the underparts. If I had seen it in the ordinary course of bird watching, I should without doubt have identified it as the cock. And indeed I think it must have been the male bird, but I feel slightly reserved on the point because of the singular absence of what text-book descriptions have given me to understand as typical female subalpines.

Whichever it was—and I feel little real doubt that it was the male—it was a singularly beautiful warbler. I thought I had seen subalpines well on the Mas des Pernes, but my view to-day at a few feet range gave me a new insight into its loveliness. Of all birds the skulking warblers are certainly best seen from a hide. Only at the nest can the subtleties of their plumage *really* be observed to advantage. For this reason I have always been at a loss to understand why active field observers do not carry light hides with them for the express purpose of seeing to best advantage these cover-loving skulkers. The stumbling-block is that it necessitates the finding of a nest, but that is surely one of the most fascinating aspects of ornithology. Once the nest is found, most of the small warblers only require about twenty minutes to accustom themselves to the presence of the hide. The reward is worth while, for the bird is seen under conditions equal almost to the inspection of the skin in the British Museum—with the all-important difference that the bird is alive.

In the field I had not appreciated to full advantage the intensity of that orange-pink throat and breast, and the white moustachial streak certainly lends an air of distinction to this smart little bird. Once again I admired the eye, the dark iris of which is surrounded by a bright red eyelid. I find cause for quarrel also with the colour of the legs. In my bird to-day these were remarkably pink. The books give varying shades of brown.

There was little else to record, except that the feeding bird ate the excreta of the chicks instead of flying away with it—the normal procedure, in my experience, with warblers.

After lunch I spent the rest of the day on my night heron. On the way down near L'Armelière 'station' over a field which had been artificially flooded there was considerable bird activity. Spotted redshanks were very numerous, as also were black-tailed godwits. I saw one wood sandpiper and two stilts. I saw too my first ashy-headed wagtail—with a very poor eye stripe. What a contrast to last year, when they abounded everywhere! But the real joy of the place were the black terns, of which there must have been at least a hundred hovering over the floods—a truly lovely sight! Truly, in dry years these small oases are bird paradises!

Two of the three night heron eggs have now hatched, and the other is chipping. The second chick had clearly only just emerged when I arrived, for the broken egg shells were still in the nest. It seems clear that the eggs hatch at about a twenty-four-hour interval. The first chick is now dry, and he is a charming little brown golliwog. The old bird was her usual stolid self. She returned quickly—and just sat. I was disappointed that she did not throw the hatched egg shells overboard, for it seems that that is how they deal with them, but, no, she sat them as well as her two chicks and one egg.

My last view of her was superb. As the footsteps of my wife came through the undergrowth, she slowly raised herself. There she posed, half standing, listening to the sound. The sun was full on her like a spotlight in a most theatrical manner. She held that pose for about two minutes, and then with a squawk leapt off the nest and perched with her feet on the bough to which my hide sacks were pinned. She was certainly not more than six inches from my head. Then she went. It was the last I saw of her.

PLATE 67. NIGHT HERON SITTING

PLATE 68. NIGHT HERON SUSPICIOUS

APPENDIX A

A BRIEF BIBLIOGRAPHICAL NOTE

FULL details of the considerable ornithological bibliography of Andalucia and Provence are to be found in the following papers:

'The Birds of Southern Spain', by the Rev. F. C. R. Jourdain (*Ibis*, 1936).

'L'Avifaune de la Camargue et des Grands Étangs voisin de Berre et de Thau', by N. Mayaud (*L'Oiseau*, 1938).

The bibliographies appended to these papers give full lists of the published written matter, both short and long, which deals with the bird life of the two deltas.

The present note has no intention of recapitulating these details, but merely calls attention to the most significant literature published on these areas. Andalucia lacks a systematic account of its bird life which is complete, modern and critical, for the Rev. F. C. R. Jourdain's paper was unfortunately never completed before his death, though it answers all requirements for the passerine birds.

The Camargue is better served, for both Mayaud's paper and the two papers of W. E. Glegg—'The Birds of L'Ile de la Camargue et la Petite Camargue' (*Ibis*, 1931), and his supplement (*Ibis*, 1941)—in their different ways give an excellent picture of the delta's bird life. Mayaud generalizes the evidence, whilst Glegg details it—but the latter's papers must be read in conjunction with one another. Reference should also be made to Dr. G. J. Van Oort and A. A. Tjittes' communication, in English, to the Dutch *Ardea* (1933)—*Ornithological Observations in the Camargue*. *The Actes de la Réserve Zoologique et Botanique de Camargue* (1930-8), the annual bulletin published by the Société Nationale d'Acclimatation, provide also a yearly commentary on the delta's bird life, which, if at times unfortunately lacking in detail, gives a picture of the annual changes and is valuable for its meteorological data—a matter of great

K   [145]

importance in any consideration of Camargue migration.

If Andalucia is less fortunate than the Camargue in its systematic lists, it is by way of compensation favoured with a fascinating literature of its own. Lt.-Col. L. H. Irby's *Ornithology of the Straits of Gibraltar* (1875) is still an invaluable guide to that region, while no ornithologist who intends to watch birds in Southern Spain can afford to miss the pleasure, almost the excitement, of reading *Wild Spain* (1893) by Abel Chapman and W. J. Buck, and again, by the same authors, *Unexplored Spain* (1910). Mention too must be made of Col. Willoughby Verner's *My Life Among the Wild Birds in Spain* (1909), perhaps the best book on pure birds-nesting ever written. The Camargue unfortunately has no such attractive commentators.

Of published bird photographs from Andalucia the most noteworthy are those of R. B. Lodge which appear scattered over the pages of his books, e.g. *Pictures of Bird Life*; of W. Farren, in the now extinct publication, *Wild Life*; of Bentley Beetham, in *Among Our Banished Birds*; and again in *Wild Life*; and of R. Atkinson, in his *Quest for the Griffon*, which in addition to magnificent photographs of this great vulture gives a most amusing account of Spanish 'red tape'. The Camargue, for reasons which in view of its accessibility are difficult to assess, has been little favoured by photographers. Glegg, however, has published a number of plates in illustration of his communications to *British Birds*, as also has the present writer in that periodical and in both *The Field* and *Country Life*. J. P. Strijbos, of Holland, has also done excellent work with his camera in this region.

Appended is a brief list of the longer and more interesting literature on these two regions.

1871. Saunders, H. 'A List of the Birds of Southern Spain', *Ibis*, pp. 54-68, 205-25, 384-402.
1875. Irby, Lt.-Col. L. H. *Ornithology of the Straits of Gibraltar* (1895—2nd edition).
1884. Chapman, A. 'Rough Notes on Spanish Ornithology', *Ibis*, pp. 66-99.
1888. Chapman, A. 'Winter Notes in Spain', *Ibis*, pp. 444-61.
1893. Chapman, A., and Buck, W. J. *Wild Spain.*
1895. Eagle Clark, W. 'On the Ornithology of the Delta of the Rhône', *Ibis*, pp. 173-211.

1898. Eagle Clark, W. 'On the Ornithology of the Delta of the Rhône', *Ibis*, pp. 465–84.

1899. Witherby, H. F. *Two Months on the Guadalquiver*.

1902. Noble, H. 'Forty-four Days' Nesting in Andalucia', *Ibis*, pp. 69–89.

1903. Lodge, R. B. *Pictures of Bird Life*, pp. 265–330.

1909. Verner, Col. W. *My Life among the Wild Birds in Spain*.

1910. Chapman, A. and Buck, W. J. *Unexplored Spain*.

1912. Lynes, Commander H. 'Bird Notes from two Andalucian Sierras', *Ibis*, pp. 454–89.

1914. Farren, W. 'A Heronry in Southern Spain', *Wild Life*, IV, pp. 200–15.

1921. Stenhouse, Surg.-Admiral, J. H. 'Bird Notes from Southern Spain', *Ibis*, pp. 573–94.

1927. Beetham, Bentley, *Among our Banished Birds*.

1931. Glegg, W. E. 'The Birds of L'Ile de la Camargue et la Petite Camargue', *Ibis*, pp. 209–41, 419–46.

1931. Gallet, L. 'Notes sur la Nidification en Camargue de l'Aigrette Garzette, du Bihoreau et du Crabier', *L'Oiseau*, pp. 54–7.

1931. Reboussin, R. 'Localisation et Associations Ornithologiques sur le Territoire de la Camargue', *L'Oiseau*, pp. 339–62.

1931. 'Actes de la Réserve Zoologique et Botanique de Camargue'. No. 1, March 1930 to No. 22, 1938. *Bull. de la Soc. Nat. d'Acc. de France*.

1933. Alexander, W. B., Harrison, T. H., Pease, H. J. R., and Tucker, B. W. 'Some Spring Observations on the Birds of the Camargue', *Ibis*, pp. 521–32.

1936. Jourdain, Rev. F. C. R. 'The Birds of Southern Spain— Part I, Passeres', *Ibis*, pp. 725–63.

1937. Jourdain, Rev. F. C. R. 'The Birds of Southern Spain— Part II, Passeres', *Ibis*, pp. 110–52.

1937. Atkinson, R. *Quest for the Griffon*.

1938. Mayaud, N. 'L'Avifaune de la Camargue et des Grands Etangs voisin de Berre et de Thau', *L'Oiseau*, pp. 2843–49.

1939. Ferrier, J. M. 'The Camargue Reserve in Southern France', *Trans. Norfolk and Norwich Nat. Soc.*, pp. 320–33.

1941. Glegg, W. E. 'The Birds of L'Ile de la Camargue et la Petite Camargue'—Supplement., *Ibis*, pp. 556–610.

APPENDIX B

SCIENTIFIC NAMES OF BIRDS MENTIONED IN TEXT

NOTE. Many species mentioned in the text are of several sub-species, in most cases only identifiable in the hand, e.g. the skylark of Provence is probably *Alauda arvensis cantarella*; that of Andalucia *Alauda arvensis sierrae*. I have therefore adopted only binomials in the following list, unless the sub-species is either identifiable in the field or is discussed as a sub-species in the text.

Raven	*Corvus corax*
Carrion Crow	*Corvus corone*
Magpie	*Pica pica*
Azure-winged Magpie	*Cyanopica cyanus*
Jay	*Garrulus glandarius*
Starling	*Sturnus vulgaris*
Spotless Starling	*Sturnus unicolor*
Golden Oriole	*Oriolus oriolus*
Hawfinch	*Coccothraustes coccothraustes*
Greenfinch	*Chloris chloris*
Goldfinch	*Carduelis carduelis*
Linnet	*Carduelis cannabina*
Serin	*Serinus canarius*
Chaffinch	*Fringilla caelebs*
House Sparrow	*Passer domesticus*
Corn Bunting	*Emberiza calandra*
Cirl Bunting	*Emberiza cirlus*
Ortolan	*Emberiza hortulana*
Calandra Lark	*Melanocorypha calandra*
Short-toed Lark	*Calandrella brachydactyla*
Marisma Lark	*Calandrella rufescens apetzii*
Crested Lark	*Galerida cristata*
Brehm's Crested Lark	*Galerida theklae*

Woodlark	*Lullula arborea*
Skylark	*Alauda arvensis*
Tawny Pipit	*Anthus campestris*
Tree Pipit	*Anthus trivialis*
Blue-headed Wagtail	*Motacilla flava flava*
Ashy-headed Wagtail	*Motacilla flava cinereocapilla*
Spanish Yellow Wagtail	*Motacilla flava iberiae*
Yellow Wagtail	*Motacilla flava flavissima*
Grey Wagtail	*Motacilla cinerea*
White Wagtail	*Motacilla alba*
Short-toed Tree Creeper	*Certhia brachydactyla*
Great Tit	*Parus major*
Blue Tit	*Parus caeruleus*
Coal Tit	*Parus ater*
Crested Tit	*Parus cristatus*
Long-tailed Tit	*Aegithalus caudatus*
Penduline Tit	*Remiz pendulinus*
Bearded Tit	*Panurus biarmicus*
South European Grey Shrike	*Lanius excubitor meridionalis*
Woodchat Shrike	*Lanius senator*
Red-backed Shrike	*Lanius collurio*
Spotted Flycatcher	*Muscicapa grisola*
Pied Flycatcher	*Muscicapa atricapilla*
Willow Warbler	*Phylloscopus trochilus*
Bonelli's Warbler	*Phylloscopus bonelli*
Wood Warbler	*Phylloscopus sibilatrix*
Cetti's Warbler	*Cettia cetti*
Moustached Warbler	*Lusciniola melanopogon*
Savi's Warbler	*Loscustella luscinioides*
Grasshopper Warbler	*Locustella naevia*
Great Reed Warbler	*Acrocephalus arundinaceus*
Reed Warbler	*Acrocephalus scirpaceus*
Sedge Warbler	*Acrocephalus schoenobaenus*
Melodious Warbler	*Hypolais polyglotta*
Orphean Warbler	*Sylvia hortensis*
Blackcap	*Sylvia atricapilla*
Whitethroat	*Sylvia communis*
Rüppell's Warbler	*Sylvia ruppelli*
Sardinian Warbler	*Sylvia melanocephala*

Subalpine Warbler	*Sylvia cantillans*
Spectacled Warbler	*Sylvia conspicillata*
Dartford Warbler	*Sylvia undata*
Rufous Warbler	*Agrobates galactotes*
Fantail Warbler	*Cisticola juncidis*
Blackbird	*Turdus merula*
Rock Thrush	*Monticola saxatilis*
Blue Rock Thrush	*Monticola solitarius*
Black-eared Wheatear	*Oenanthe hispanica*
Black Wheatear	*Oenanthe levcura*
Whinchat	*Saxicola rubetra*
Stonechat	*Saxicola torquata*
Redstart	*Phoenicurus phoenicurus*
Black Redstart	*Phoenicurus ochrurus*
Nightingale	*Luscinia megarhynca*
Swallow	*Hirundo rustica*
House Martin	*Delichon urbica*
Sand Martin	*Riparia riparia*
Alpine Swift	*Micropus melba*
Swift	*Micropus apus*
Pallid Swift	*Micropus murinus*
Bee-eater	*Merops apiaster*
Hoopoe	*Upupa epops*
Roller	*Coracias garrulus*
Kingfisher	*Alcedo atthis*
Green Woodpecker	*Picus viridis*
Wryneck	*Jynx torquilla*
Cuckoo	*Cuculus canorus*
Great Spotted Cuckoo	*Clamator glandarius*
Eagle Owl	*Bubo bubo*
Scops Owl	*Otus scops*
Little Owl	*Athene noctua*
Lanner Falcon	*Falco biarmicus*
Hobby Falcon	*Falco subbuteo*
Red-footed Falcon	*Falco vespertinus*
Kestrel	*Falco tinnunculus*
Lesser Kestrel	*Falco naumanni*
Imperial Eagle	*Aquila heliaca*
Bonelli's Eagle	*Hieraëtus fasciatus*

Booted Eagle	*Hieraëtus pennatus*
Buzzard	*Buteo buteo*
Marsh Harrier	*Circus aeruginosus*
Montagu's Harrier	*Circus pygarus*
Sparrow Hawk	*Accipiter nisus*
Red Kite	*Milvus milvus*
Black Kite	*Milvus migrans*
Osprey	*Pandion haliaëtus*
Egyptian Vulture	*Neophron percnopterus*
Griffon Vulture	*Gyps fulvus*
White Stork	*Ciconia ciconia*
Spoonbill	*Platalea leucorodia*
Common Heron	*Ardea cinerea*
Purple Heron	*Ardea purpurea*
Little Egret	*Egretta garzetta*
Buff-backed Heron	*Ardeola ibis*
Squacco Heron	*Ardeola ralloides*
Night Heron	*Nycticorax nycticorax*
Little Bittern	*Ixobrychus minutus*
Bittern	*Botaurus stellaris*
Flamingo	*Phoenicopterus ruber*
Ruddy Shelduck	*Casarca feruginea*
Mallard	*Anas platyrhyncha*
Gadwall	*Anas strepera*
Teal	*Anas crecca*
Garganey	*Anas querquedula*
Widgeon	*Anas penelope*
Pintail	*Anas acuta*
Shoveler	*Spatula clypeata*
Red-crested Pochard	*Netta rufina*
Common Pochard	*Aythya ferina*
Ferruginous Duck	*Aythya nyroca*
Tufted Duck	*Aythya fuligula*
White-headed Duck	*Oxyura leucocephala*
Great Crested Grebe	*Podiceps cristatus*
Black-necked Grebe	*Podiceps nigricollis*
Little Grebe	*Podiceps ruficollis*
Wood Pigeon	*Columba palumbus*
Turtle Dove	*Streptopelia turtur*

Black-bellied Sand Grouse	*Pterocles orientalis*
Pin-tailed Sand Grouse	*Pterocles alchata*
Bar-tailed Godwit	*Limosa lapponica*
Black-tailed Godwit	*Limosa limosa*
Curlew	*Numenius arquata*
Whimbrel	*Numenius phaeopus*
Common Snipe	*Capella gallinago*
Dunlin	*Calidris alpina*
Curlew-Sandpiper	*Calidris testacea*
Little Stint	*Calidris minuta*
Sanderling	*Crocethia alba*
Ruff	*Philomachus pugnax*
Common Sandpiper	*Actitis hypoleucos*
Wood Sandpiper	*Tringa glareola*
Green Sandpiper	*Tringa ochropus*
Redshank	*Tringa totanus*
Spotted Redshank	*Tringa erythropus*
Greenshank	*Tringa nebularia*
Ringed Plover	*Charadrius hiaticula*
Little Ringed Plover	*Charadrius dubius*
Kentish Plover	*Leucopolius alexandrinus*
Golden Plover	*Pluvialis apricaria*
Grey Plover	*Squatarola squatarola*
Lapwing	*Vanellus vanellus*
Black-winged Stilt	*Himantopus himantopus*
Avocet	*Recurvirostra avosetta*
Oyster-Catcher	*Haematopus ostralegus*
Pratincole	*Glareola pratincola*
Stone Curlew	*Burhinus oedicnemus*
Great Bustard	*Otis tarda*
Little Bustard	*Otis tetrax*
Common Crane	*Grus grus*
Black Tern	*Childonis niger*
Whiskered Tern	*Chlidonias hybrida*
Gull-billed Tern	*Gelochelidon nilotica*
Caspian Tern	*Hydroprogne caspia*
Common Tern	*Sterna hirundo*
Little Tern	*Sterna albifrons*
Black-headed Gull	*Larus ridiundus*

Mediterranean Herring Gull	*Larus argentatus michahellis*
Lesser Black-backed Gull	*Larus fuscus*
Slender-billed Gull	*Larus gelastes*
Moorhen	*Gallinula chloropus*
Purple Gallinule	*Porphyrio caeruleus*
Coot	*Fulica atra*
Crested Coot	*Fulica cristata*
Red-legged Partridge	*Alectoris rufa*

APPENDIX C

FRENCH NAMES OF CAMARGUE BIRDS

Avocet	*Avocette*
Bittern	*Butor étoile*
Bittern, Little	*Blongios naine*
Bunting, Corn	*Bruant proyer*
Bunting, Ortolan	*Bruant ortolan*
Coot, Common	*Foulque macroule*
Creeper, Short-toed Tree	*Grimpereau brachydactyle*
Crow, Carrion	*Corneille noir*
Cuckoo	*Coucou*
Curlew, Common	*Courlis cendré*
Curlew, Stone	*Oidicnème criard*
Duck, Tufted	*Canard morillon*
Eagle, Bonelli's	*Aigle de Bonelli*
Egret, Little	*Aigrette garzette*
Flamingo	*Flamant*
Flycatcher, Pied	*Gobe-mouche noir*
Gadwall	*Canard chipeau*
Garganey	*Sarcelle d'été*
Godwit, Bar-tailed	*Barge rousse*
Godwit, Black-tailed	*Barge à queue noir*
Goldfinch	*Chardonneret élégant*
Grebe, Great Crested	*Grèbe huppé*
Grebe, Little	*Grèbe castagneux*
Greenfinch	*Verdier d'Europe*
Gull, Black-headed	*Mouette rieuse*
Gull, Mediterranean Herring	*Goéland argent à pieds jaunes*
Harrier, Marsh	*Buse harpaye*
Heron, Common	*Héron cendré*
Heron, Night	*Héron bihoreau*

Heron, Purple	*Héron pourpré*
Heron, Squacco	*Héron crabier*
Hobby	*Faucon hobereau*
Hoopoe	*Huppé*
Kingfisher	*Martin pêcheur*
Kite, Black	*Milan noir*
Lapwing	*Vanneau huppé*
Lark, Crested	*Cochévis huppé*
Lark, Calandra	*Alouette calandre*
Lark, Short-toed	*Alouette calandrelle*
Lark, Sky-	*Alouette des champs*
Linnet	*Linotte des cignes*
Magpie	*Pie bavarde*
Mallard	*Canard col-vert*
Moorhen	*Poule d'eau*
Nightingale	*Rossignol philomèle*
Oriole, Golden	*Loriot*
Osprey	*Balbuzard fluviatile*
Owl, Little	*Chouette chevêche*
Owl, Sceps	*Hibou petit-duc*
Oyster-Catcher	*Huitrier-pie*
Partridge, Red-legged	*Perdrix rouge*
Pintail	*Canard pilet*
Pipit, Tawny	*Pipit rousseline*
Pipit, Tree	*Pipit des arbres*
Plover, Kentish	*Pluvier à collier interrompu*
Plover, Little Ringed	*Petit pluvier à collier*
Pochard, Common	*Canard milouin*
Pochard, Red-crested	*Brante roussâtre*
Pratincole	*Glaréole à cottier*
Redshank	*Chevalier gambette*
Roller	*Rollier*
Ruff	*Chevalier arlequin*
Serin	*Serin cini*
Shoveler	*Canard souchet*
Shrike, Woodchat	*Pie-grièche rousse*
Snipe, Common	*Bécassine des marais*
Sparrow, House	*Moineau domestique*
Stilt, Black-winged	*Echasse blanc*

Stonechat	*Tarier rubicole*
Swallow	*Hirondelle*
Swift, Common	*Martinet noir*
Teal	*Sarcelle d'hiver*
Tern, Black	*Guiffette épouvantaille*
Teal, Common	*Sterne Pierre-Garin*
Teal, Gull-billed	*Sterne nansel*
Tern, Little	*Sterne naine*
Tern, Whiskered	*Gruffette moustac*
Thrush, Rock	*Merle de roche*
Tit, Bearded	*Mésange à moustaches*
Tit, Coal	*Mésange noir*
Tit, Long-tailed	*Mésange à longue queue*
Tit, Penduline	*Mésange remiz*
Vulture, Egyptian	*Vautour percnoptère*
Wagtail, Blue-headed	*Bergeronette printanière*
Warbler, Cetti's	*Bouscarle de Cetti*
Warbler, Dartford	*Fauvette pitchou*
Warbler, Fantail	*Cisticole des joncs*
Warbler, Great Reed	*Rousserole turdoide*
Warbler, Melodious	*Hippolaïs polyglotte*
Warbler, Moustached	*Amnicole à moustaches noires*
Warbler, Orphean	*Fauvette orphée*
Warbler, Reed	*Rousserole effarvatte*
Warbler, Sardinian	*Fauvette mélanocéphale*
Warbler, Spectacled	*Fauvette à lunettes*
Warbler, Subalpine	*Fauvette passerinette*
Wheatear, Black-eared	*Tarquet stapazin*
Widgeon	*Canard siffleur*
Wryneck	*Torcol fourmilier*

INDEX

Avocet, 35, 38–9, 42, 74, 95, 98, 103, 124

Bee-eater, 20, 21
Bittern, 90
  Little, 99
Blackbird, 19
Bunting, Cirl, 57
  Corn, 20, 24, 69, 116
  Ortolan, 40, 73, 123, 131
Bustard, Great, 55
  Little, 52–3
Buzzard, Common, 43, 46, 52, 54, 123, 138, 141

Chaffinch, 54, 121
Coot, 25, 42, 59, 73
  Crested, 61
Crane, 22
Creeper, Short-toed Tree, 54, 134
Crow, Carrion, 103
Cuckoo, 85, 123, 138
  Great Spotted, 42
Curlew, Common, 35, 124
  Stone, 43, 73, 85, 126

Duck, Ferruginous, 58, 61
  Ruddy Sheld-, 42, 43
  Tufted, 42
  White-headed, 42, 43, 61
Dunlin, 37, 38, 39, 103

Eagle, Bonelli's, 30, 32, 34, 54, 105, 128
  Booted, 48, 54
  Imperial, 43, 48
Egret, Little, 35, 37, 42, 49, 58, 60, 71, 74–6, 78–9, 80–2, 86–7, 89, 99, 116, 124

Falcon, Lanner, 47, 48
  Red-footed, 105
Flamingo, 38–9, 40, 42, 78, 94, 96, 98, 103, 116, 130
Flycatcher, Pied, 73, 78, 85, 96, 98, 132
  Spotted, 104

Gadwall, 42
Gallinule, Purple, 61
Garganey, 42, 74
Godwit, Bar-tailed, 37, 131
  Black-tailed, 39, 42, 73–4, 86
Goldfinch, 70, 83, 116
Grebe, Black-necked, 42
  Great Crested, 74
  Little, 25, 42, 82, 90
Greenfinch, 129
Greenshank, 39, 73, 74, 131
Gull, Black-headed, 37, 39, 71, 98
  Lesser Black-backed, 102, 124
  Mediterranean Herring, 71, 98, 124
  Slender-billed, 41

Harrier, Marsh, 22, 27–8, 35, 59, 71, 84, 107, 116, 124
  Montagu's, 24, 27, 35, 39, 84, 105, 111, 116
Hawfinch, 134
Hawk, Sparrow, 134
Heron, Buff-backed, 19, 20, 24, 35, 42, 45, 49, 56–65, 101
  Common, 37, 101, 106
  Night, 46, 49, 60, 79, 80, 82, 87, 89, 117, 127–8, 132, 134, 137–42, 144
  Purple, 28, 71, 73, 85, 107, 116, 132
Hobby, 47, 71, 72, 132
Hoopoe, 49, 54, 73, 83, 88, 90–3, 96, 99, 100, 105, 116, 134

Jay, 121

Kestrel, 52, 54, 73, 116
  Lesser, 23
Kingfisher, 91
Kite, Black, 24, 29, 37, 39, 43, 46, 52, 54, 139, 141
  Red, 43, 47

Lapwing, 39, 77, 107, 124

[157]

INDEX